MOTHER OF EIGHT SURVIVES POPULATION EXPLOSION

Roxane —

Our experience are
meant to benefit
our fellow wanderers
on this planet — Enjoy
all your experiences —

Marilyn 5-9-15

MOTHER OF EIGHT

SURVIVES

POPULATION

EXPLOSION

"Just Between Us"
newspaper column selections

Marilyn Catherine McDonald, MA

To order additional copies of this book, contact:
Xlibris Corporation
1-888-795-4274
www.Xlibris.com
Orders@Xlibris.com
21176

This book is dedicated to my eight children:

Diane, Thomas, Carol, Sheila,
Teresa, Paul, Mary and Christina.

They give my life true, enduring meaning and joy.

If one advances confidently in the direction of his dreams, and endeavors to live the life which he has imagined, he will meet with a success unexpected in common hours.
Henry David Thoreau (1817-1862)

CONTENTS

V. PURSUING HEALTH, WEALTH AND HAPPINESS

VI. PREACHING WHAT WE PRACTICE

ACKNOWLEDGEMENTS

In the 1970s, writing a weekly personal column about almost anything I had on my mind gave me a forum for a variety of viewpoints. I appreciate the opportunity provided me by the former *Community Press* in Portland, Oregon. The newspaper reached into several communities, and I wrote primarily for the West Side Edition. This advertising-supported paper was delivered free to all households. I wrote hundreds of features and profiles in addition to nearly 200 columns.

A special thanks goes to Spencer Heinz, a helpful *Community Press* editor who later went on to the *Oregonian* daily newspaper.

All of my eight children were living at home during the time I wrote the "Just Between Us" column, and they were my greatest inspiration. I am who I am today because of how we all grew up together.

The Seventies were years of political turmoil, as well as personal problems for me with a failing marriage that ended in divorce in 1977. Then, following 22 years as a single-parent I married my daughter Sheila's widower father-in-law. My husband, Harry Taylor, has read every word of this manuscript, and his corrections and input have been most welcome and valuable.

Of the many, many writer friends who have encouraged me for decades, I treasure guidance provided by Norma Upson.

Many thanks go to Lendon H. Smith, MD, who reviewed the majority of this book in manuscript form in 1976. He wrote the foreword and gave me an introduction to his editor at Prentice Hall, Inc.

Tam Mossman, Senior Editor for the Trade Book Division wrote me the most wonderful rejection letter that read in part:

"My thanks to you and Dunny Smith for letting me
see your manuscript, *JUST BETWEEN US*. I most certainly
believe in your writing. Your learning is always apt and
relevant, your observations pithy and original, and your
questions ones that most of us should have been asking long
ago."

Unfortunately, or fortunately, I put the manuscript away and
got busy with other career and family matters. Dr. Smith passed
on to his reward November 17, 2001. I hope his family and friends
can appreciate the honor I pay him by using his foreword.

And, thanks to the people who brought us the wonderful world
of Internet and the computer/electronic technology that make book
publishing so much more affordable and accessible.

FOREWORD

If you are a human being, you will like this book. If you have a short attention span (as I do), you will like this book. Marilyn does not solve many problems about day to day living, but she communicates the feeling, "I've been there. You will survive also, and when you look back you will see the joys." It is not a HOW TO book, but a way to compare your own human emotions with a reliable human standard, Marilyn.

Nobody ever believes that "they were married and lived happily ever after." While he/she is living through the busy child rearing years, there seem to be more downs than ups. But once it is history one must concede it was a human time. Without the pains, sorrows, frustrations and disappointments, one cannot realize the joys of growing. Adults grow, too, as Marilyn points out.

Marilyn knows we are all floating along the stream of life, trapped to a certain extent by our bodies, our talents and our past follies, but she gives us all an oar or two to alter the course. It is an optimistic book, but not a sickeningly sweet-keep-smiling-and-all-will-be-OK book. She feels we are all growing and have the capacity of change for the better. Hope is there but we have to row a bit.

This book is a statement of philosophy. We are social human beings and we must interact with other social human beings. If you can laugh and smile more than you cry and frown, you are a social human being.

—Lendon H. Smith (Reviewed manuscript 25 Sept. '76)
   June 3rd, 1921-November 17th, 2001

Author of:

The Children's Doctor	*Encyclopedia of Baby and Child Care*
New Wives' Tales	*Improving Your Child's Behavior Chemistry*
Dr. Smith's Low Stress Diet	*Dr. Smith's Diet Plan for Teenagers*
Happiness is a Healthy Life	*Ho to Raise a Healthy Child*

INTRODUCTION

The majority of this book was originally assembled in 1975-76, after my column "Just Between Us" finished its weekly three-and a-half-year run in the *Community Press*, Portland, Oregon.

Several years ago, at Christmas, I gave each of my eight adult children binders with copies of the incomplete manuscript I am about to share with you. They enjoyed searching for "their stories." They were all a huge part of what I did and why I did it.

The 1960s and 1970s were times of tremendous turmoil and change in our society. It was all about Vietnam, human freedom, liberation, conservation, Zero Population Growth, and saving the earth for future generations. With eight children, I was living in the midst of my own population explosion—and turning heads whenever I packed them all with me into a restaurant or grocery store.

Those were challenging times, interesting and fun times. This book speaks to life's challenges, the search for human freedom and spiritual growth. Putting one foot in front of the other on a daily basis.

For decades, we sang and we cheered for personal liberty and freedom from war—but no one can be totally liberated. Every individual has commitments to honor.

Freedom is a mental attitude, and being liberated is about half way between where you've been and where you'd like to be. It denotes progress. A sense of travel. In effect, you might say you're on a trip. Reaching plateaus along the way where you rest and then continue on.

Don't expect children to understand you, the job you do, or the sacrifices you make. They thought you were senile about the time they reached the age of reason. Their conviction strengthens as they grow older and begin taking sociology and psychology courses in college. They may even use you as a term project in the study of abnormal behavior. You'll have to contend with their "good advice" when they reach adulthood. And when you, sad to say, are on the decline.

Come, and share with me the big and little things that make life worth living.

I

SWIMMING UPSTREAM

In the process of reaching adulthood, the admirable Columbia River salmon determinedly swims upstream against great odds to return to the place of birth—to spawn and die. Whether salmon proceed knowingly or unknowingly, their sense of purpose and accomplishment lead us to hope that humans also possess some of that same sense of purpose—driving us forward to meet our daily challenges. Someday, we hope to look back with a feeling of relief and release—with the realization that it was worth the effort.

Winning the rat-race with seconds

"Be the first on your block to own a new this. Be the first in your ladies club or church to wear a new that."

There's a struggle for the first place in line, first in a game, first to speak and first to leave. Space is limited for number ones.

When I was growing up (I still am) I learned a trick of calling out "second" or "third" when the games started because everyone else was getting hung up on "first." For me, it took the pressure off game playing.

We live in a competitive society where being number one is extremely important. Sports fans are less interested in reading the newspaper to find out who is number two. It's a case of who's leading the pack.

School reports come out and we scan the results to see if our protégés are on top, leading their peers. Even the little ones push and pull to get to the top of the heap.

Is it any wonder there are dropouts? The pace gets quicker all the time and the prizes go to the swift—to those who excel. If you come in a close second you may be rewarded but soon forgotten, even though the margin was slim.

We've heard the saying "It's not whether you win or lose but how you play the game that counts." That may be true on a subjective level, but just listen to all the objective minded people around us are telling us what we should have done to win, where we goofed.

Children are bombarded with criticism at their sports events. Well-meaning parents are waiting to tell them what the winner did to gain the advantage, and what the loser did that he shouldn't have done. Kids know when they haven't done well, and nagging doesn't help their self-image.

Perhaps we Americans are more obsessed with newness and firsts than citizens of other countries because of our material advances, and technological and scientific progress. Our pace is rapid to acquire more than the necessities of life.

The excitement for newness extends beyond the material items of life into the less tangible areas. "We must, of course, update our thinking, in keeping with the times," is a well-worn phrase in any century. As a result of trying to keep up or become number one we may be abandoning useful traditions and values along with yesterday's newspaper and last week's garbage.

Consumer-producer roles

As we sat at the table finishing our meal, one of the children asked, "What's a consumer?"

Before I could answer, our 11-year-old said, "That's a taxpayer's children."

My husband and I exchanged bewildered glances and I asked, "Where did you hear that?"

She didn't know where she got the idea, and I began to ponder the effectiveness of our socialization mechanism. The consumer-producer battle, or relationship, has been going on for decades, and the concept of women and children as consumers and men as producers has seeped into the value system.

Women once took pride in their role as producers of human beings, and contributors to the common good by the care and feeding of children. Now the trend is for a person's contributions to be measured in terms of how much money their products or services are worth on the open market.

I think it is an unfortunate turn of events that women also have swallowed the value system that places dollar signs on the worth of a human being. When you ask a man what he's worth he'll tell you in hundreds of thousands or millions of dollars. When you ask a woman she may get a puzzled look on her face.

The Internal Revenue Service knows what we're worth in dollars and cents, but do we know our real worth on the open market?

If you judge individual value by dollars, how do you judge? What are the criteria?

You can't base a person's value entirely on need. Someone needs them today, but what about tomorrow? Tomorrow they may be in the way. Tomorrow they may be a burden.

So often, I've heard a woman say she is "just a housewife" when asked what she does. The term says nothing in their favor as contributors to the whole social picture, and they usually are apologetic for their deficiency.

If a woman was the manager of a sanitarium or a hospital, and being paid accordingly, she would reap the social benefits of respect. But, put the same woman in charge of a house full if flu-bugged children and she receives no notice, reward or respect from society.

To some extent, a woman may itch to get out of her house and go to work to prove she has value. She finds she can no longer gauge her worth in housework, hot meals and kids' in clean clothes. She finds herself trying to be superwoman and pressing beyond the limits of her endurance.

Often women must work outside the home to make ends meet. And, not all women are meant to be "stay-at-home moms."

Are children consumers until they are gainfully employed?

What do they contribute toward the advancement and benefit of society? Are they merely sponges to absorb our way of life?

Attitudes toward answering these questions may give us a clue to the ever-widening generation gaps.

It's a Band-Aid world

"Keep out of the reach of children," warnings are promptly heeded when viewed on the containers of potentially dangerous substances.

Sometimes I think it would be a good idea to put a similar warning on Band-Aid boxes. When you need one they've all disappeared. Children have come to the conclusion that a ready-made bandage has many uses—not always connected with cuts or scrapes.

When the homey little gesture of "Let Mother kiss it and make it all better," proved minimally effective I switched to the placebo of the Band-Aid. The kids feel a cure come upon them, the crying stops, and I go along with the gag.

Now, this Band-Aid generation can't seem to keep their hands off the box.

When they run out of cellophane tape (that's another one that disappears fast) they have been known to use Band-Aids for entering pictures in a school project book. They have even tried to patch plastic balls, swimming pools and air mattresses with Band-Aids.

One of the girls has been using adhesive tape to plaster down her ringlets at night Ouch! That hurts when you pull it off in the morning. I'm sure she'd be using Band-Aids if we weren't out of them.

I discovered we were out of Band-Aids when I needed one to close a bleeding cut on Tina's (age 2) finger. She cut it while rummaging through the waste basket and discovered the shiny jagged-edged lid from a tin can.

Tina's different. She doesn't like bandages on her fingers. After she chewed the adhesive tape off three times I gave up and the finger stopped bleeding by itself with a little help from the adhesive residue.

It's the little things that make life so frustrating. Like being out of Band-Aids when you need one; or when you can't find the new bottle of glue or roll of cellophane tape. And, no matter how many pencils you buy there isn't one available to write down a phone message, or else the lead is broken.

Bouncing the crystal ball

At the risk of having occultists stick pins in a voo doo doll bearing my name, I'll give my thoughts on the psychic phenomenon movement.

I'm convinced it will be around for a long time. I'm also convinced there's a "sucker born every minute," and someone out there willing to take his ready cash, by hook or by crook.

There will always be people looking for a short cut to living, an escape out of the present and into the future by delving into the world of things yet-to-come.

We constantly are being made aware of the impact of this psychic movement, and persons claiming to have special "powers" are more than willing to help us direct our lives for a fee ranging from hundreds to thousands of dollars. They are more than willing to share their futuristic insights with you—for a price. All sales are based on supply and demand. And, all sales are final.

Why are people becoming more interested in psychic phenomenon? Why are the youth adopting the mysticism of the Oriental religions and the occultism of the ancients?

Is it because excitement with the known has reached saturation level and young and old are looking for new worlds to explore? Is it perhaps a rejection of the familiar because it has proven to be a disillusionment?

Where do you go when there doesn't seem to be anywhere left to go? Perhaps many people are feeling a dead-end in their lives; searching for new avenues and approaches to personal success;

drawing more on their inner resources and looking for new strengths, supports and experiences.

There are so many conflicting philosophies around that a person can pick and choose to suit himself. People are claiming that religion is a crutch and are reaching out for other crutches, becoming addicted to their new awareness, new philosophy—anything new.

Since the Society for Psychical Research was formed in England in 1882, there has been one sweeping discovery regarding the "mind and matter has power beyond what is known" premise. That is, there is a vast area of disagreement. Although a great may examples of spiritual abilities exist there is minimal agreement on the "how and why" of it all.

People are curious by nature. The future is mysterious and some have a need to know what will take place. A good student of history can make some pretty sound educated guesses about the outcome of the world events in the future, but others need to know more. They go to the spiritualists for fortune telling, mind reading, studied premonitions, getting their haunted house analyzed, talking with the dead, reading their stars, studying the numbers in their lives, and all manner of approaches to satisfying their curiosity.

I have been to psychic fairs and had my aura, my palm and my handwriting read. I also have a computer printout detailing my past lives. I don't totally discount psychic phenomenon, but on the other hand I'm not preaching or promoting the same. Truth is everywhere.

Scientists reject most areas of psychic phenomenon. Astronomers do not believe in astrology and mathematicians doubt the value of numerology.

Personally, I can't see the value of going from a "dead end" feeling to a "locked in" feeling. If you allow yourself to be ruled by the stars, the numbers in your life, your circumstances, your fate, or your future as foretold by a seer, you may be robbing yourself of your own free will. Trust in you ability to do something for yourself, your ambition, and your money.

It's true that the human being has more resources and powers within his own person than he has yet discovered, and needs tools to find ways of using this inner strength. It is also true that a person can gain a great deal of strength from those around him—and the power above him or outside him. Everyone has a vocabulary for describing this power source. In my vocabulary, it's God, or Higher Power.

Excuse me if I'm somewhat skeptical when individuals claim special powers, hidden insights, views into the future, and are more than willing to be paid well for their services. I prefer to subscribe to a spiritual belief that has "revealed its secrets even to the little ones," a belief that shows you where to find the tools to deal effectively with the present. And, one that leaves me with the dignity of my free will and choices directed toward a future, and better way of life.

Are great numbers of people reverting back to the ancient practice of sun worship? Evolutionary minded biologists tell us that the sun is the source of all energy and the rest of the worlds and life are a spin-off from the sun. Some of the occultists speak of regenerating universal force, the source of all power upon which all life draws. Do we stop with the energy of the sun, or go beyond to the source of the sun's energy?

Tale of a liberated woman

Marvela Xellent took her husband to dinner. As they linger over a second cup of coffee and desert she informs him of the wonderful opportunity for advancement that just opened up for her, in *her* career field.

Husband Xellent has been broadminded and generous, encouraging his talented wife to pursue her education and career in business administration. They celebrated with a bottle of champagne each time she advanced in management.

Meanwhile, their two-and-a-third (the average) children were cared for in nursery school and on into primary, intermediate and secondary school. Cared for by people very talented in their professions. Over the years Husband X also advanced in his profession, has an established lucrative practice, and is at his peak earning time. Life is very comfortable for this average American family. Everyone sort of takes care of himself.

Now comes the blow. The wife's chance for advancement means moving the entire family to another state. "It's the chance of a lifetime," she explains.

"But, I have an established practice in this city as a professional man," he retorts.

"You've always encouraged me," she replies, "now you're not willing to make this small sacrifice."

"*Small* sacrifice?" he raises his voice, "You're asking me to move away from all my friends and business associates—the Rotary, my business, my income—and you call that *small*? And the children have you given them a thought in this matter? Candy is going to graduate from Sunrise High next year, and Bozo just made the first string on the football team, to say nothing about little You-Know-Who."

"I'm sure the children can adjust," she said with confidence. "After all they have always been very flexible, haven't they? And you shouldn't have any trouble setting up a practice again. With the raise and perks I'm getting, we can manage on my income for more than a year. You know that I'll be making as much as the man next door."

"I'm not married to the man next door," Husband X shouts, "I'm married to you and I think my professional position should be considered first."

"Why would you think that?" She quietly asks.

He grew silent. It wasn't because he made more money than she did. After taxes and overhead, he knew she came out far ahead of him with her paycheck. He couldn't use that old argument about "wives being subject to their husbands." That went out when "Lib" came in. "Let's order a drink," he slyly said in desperation, "and we'll talk about it some more after a good night's sleep."

He had one last hope. To get her to reconsider under the

influence of alcohol and "sweet talk"—the only weapons he had left, unless he could convince the children to cry.

We've been living in a nation where top executives have moved back and forth across the country for decades. It has become an accepted way of life. Advancement often involves a move or more travel.

Many a wife has tearfully made a move and learned to love her new environment. I can't quite see the shoe on the other foot. Except in rare cases.

There are an increasing number of top-notch women executives. Married women, widows, singles and divorced women are moving up the management and CEO ladder. They deserve equal pay and are assuming more hectic schedules, headaches and ulcer producing situations.

While some people look forward to a shorter work week, those with proven executive skills are much in demand and long work days and weeks will be the rule rather than the exception.

No repeats, please!

We sometimes wonder, if we had it to do over again would we do it differently. One of the areas I often wonder about is the matter of child raising.

When my eight children were all past the age of three I decided it would be safe to take a course in human development (child psychology).

I was a book addict before our first was born. Dr. Spock was the household word then, and I was going to show everyone what a good mother I could be by following his friendly advice. Like most new mothers, I thumbed through the pages when the little one was asleep, trying to anticipate her next move. It didn't take long to discover that she was always ahead or behind where the book said she would be.

When it supposedly was time, Dr. Spock, and my mother, told me to take the baby's bottle away and let her cry until she fell asleep. After a few days of that, I put the good doctor and his book away, never to open those pages again. I started depending on that vague thing we call instinct. That's another name for trial and error. There aren't two children (not even in the same family) who will let you raise them the same. Somehow they have instincts, too. They begin to rebel when your methods of operation aren't working.

During the child psychology class I began feeling like a mother hen. We split the class into small groups, mulling over mothering.

"You've been there. You can help us," one of the young ladies said to me. And I remembered how I picked the brains of older women when I faced the adult world of motherhood for the first time.

There are people willing to learn from the mistakes and successes of others. The future mothers of America have more book sources to confuse them than ever before. It takes a great deal of sorting to pick the methods that best suit the person.

I suppose it may even come about in the future that developmental psychologists will be able to find a communication going on between the mother and child even before birth.

The more I read about the child rearing process, the more I'm convinced that mothers should depend on their instincts more than they do. So much of what is being discovered was already know by my grandmothers without ever picking up a rule book on raising children.

Not that there isn't something to be learned from the books, but why get hung up on someone's clinical analysis of how monkey mothers nurture their young when you are knee deep in situations involving human children.

With the infant experiences behind me I find it more interesting studying child psychology. I remember what it was like trying to apply book knowledge to my first born. I didn't impress anyone, least of all the baby.

*   *   *

When I was the proud mother of seven children I patiently waited for the proper opening during a conversation with a group of professional people. When asked what my profession might be, I blurted out, "Oh! I'm a professional mother." In an attempt to lower raised eyebrows I quickly added, "On second thought, I'm not sure that sounds quite decent."

Make room for optimism

I returned to the college campus as a full-time student when I was well past 30, and the active Vietnam protest movement was ebbing.

I had years of political involvement, campaign and precinct work behind me, trying to arouse the sleeping populace to some level of concern over creeping, crippling bureaucracy. When we moved to Oregon from the southern California political hotbed, I was advised to cool my crusading fervor.

As I set my books down on the cafeteria table and started into my chicken soup between Psychology and American Literature classes, I heard a man's voice booming over the public address.

Between noodles, I heard something about "involvement." The speaker was pleading urgently for all of us to rise up from our apathy and get involved.

"What the h____ is he talking about?" I blurted out to the head bent over a Psychology book across the table.

"I don't know, but he's driving me wild," was the irritated reply.

Maybe when you are an over-30 college student you lose some of that zest for action. Just being there full-time, doing homework, plus taking care of a large family, plus being a freelance writer-photographer was about all the involvement I could handle.

I'm grateful that the youth are penetrating the important issues of the day, but as often happens there is considerably more heat than light generated.

Everyone has a pet issue. Bulletin boards are loaded with campaign literature, reminders of future events and coming attractions. We must be selective.

A table by the door is spread with Socialist Party literature. The next day McGovern for President people will occupy the space. A student wearing sunglasses carries an ad board over his shoulders and a tin cup in his hand. He rattles the coins in the cup, telling us not to be politically blind—vote for his candidate.

As you hurry from one class to another, a member of a student environmental interest group hands out a piece of literature on one side and the Campus Crusade for Christ gets you from the other.

Perhaps all the activism is a natural outgrowth from the pessimism gathered in the classrooms.

Biology tells us that people are too many, food is too little, and air, land and water are on their way out.

Psychology proves to us that more neurotics are walking on our streets and pushing supermarket carts than ever before.

Sociology has a hand basket full of problems. Too much power in the wrong places, too little interpersonal relationships on a meaningful level, too late to stop the industrial revolution, no way to handle the information glut, and too soon to die.

History is full of mistakes and failures appearing forebodingly familiar in our present—and we haven't learned a thing from fallen civilizations.

Philosophy tells us that nothing is absolute, everything is relative, and you only really exist in your own experience. There is no God, because everyone is god.

Life is difficult for a person of faith, but holding on to that faith during four years of college can prove terrifically challenging. The norm is relativity, as well as pragmatism and near panic.

"We must do something before it's too late!" peels the cry of alarm from all sides. Defeat and discouragement give rise to pacifism. Stopping short one day and looking around at the flurry of activity we're involved in can also be a rude awakening. We may discover we're part of the problem rather than part of the solution.

I'm not convinced that an increase in the percentage of voter turnout will ever solve our nation's or our communities' problems.

Although I believe that individuals should take the privilege of casting their votes seriously—getting more bodies into the voting booths of America doesn't guarantee an intelligent electorate.

It's easy to be pessimistic. There's plenty of good hard data to solidify that position. Optimism is what takes courage. Finding an element of hope in the dismal occurrence of every day political-governmental effort, recognizing the quantity and quality of contributions made by others, realizing the importance of our part (though small) in the whole network of events—these are necessary for survival in any kind of political structure.

*   *   *

I was riding the "Down" escalator in a crowded department store when an elderly lady behind me admired my three-year-old daughter asleep in my arms.

I told her that the child was the youngest of eight.

"My dear," she said, "how can you bring so many children into such a terrible world?"

"I hope to raise my children to make it a better world," was my response.

New lease (loan) on life

I have a whole new outlook on life. At least while I'm driving. We finally broke down and traded in the six-year-old brown station wagon on a 12-passenger brown and white van. I've been running shuttle bus service for years, and now I have the right equipment to do the job—plenty of room for everybody, and the dog, and groceries to boot.

It's sad to give up an old car that has given many years of good service. Especially when it's paid for. It's just like getting rid of an old and comfortable pair of shoes for the new pair of shoes that takes breaking in. When they drove my auto away I had to look the other way. We had been through 73,000 miles together, and I had grown attached.

But now, that is past and life goes on in the auto industry. Not only did we acquire substantial monthly payments—we also gained space and visibility, and hopefully, durability.

When you get a new car you suddenly develop the vision to see many more like yours on the road. It's the buyer's self-defense mechanism, proving to ourselves that we made a wise choice because so many others made the same choice.

We didn't believe that the van was shorter than the station wagon until we saw the proof in our own garage. Looks can be terribly deceiving.

I now know how truck drivers feel when they are sitting on the top of traffic. Looking down on little autos gives me a sense of superiority and power.

I can think of only one parallel in my life when I had this experience of seeing the world in a new way. The day I got my eyeglasses I went to a movie with friends and marveled at the clarity of the picture on the screen. For years I sat in the front row, through double features, with a false sense of security. I was nearsighted and passed all the eye tests until I reached college (the first time around right out of high school).

I tell people, don't cheat on eye tests. I didn't realize I couldn't see. My world was fuzzy and I thought everyone else lived in a fuzzy world, too. I was a good student but grew up squinting and having headaches. So, when I saw the clear outlines of figures in the movie for the first time it came as a shock.

Now, I'm seeing the world outside in a new way, somewhat similar, because of the increased visibility. I can pull right up to an intersection and see in all directions. It's beautiful. I can see my way in and out of situations I never believed possible (all but the garage, that will always be my bugaboo).

In a 12-passenger van, I can put the rival siblings in separate rows, seat-belt them in, and not worry about them getting physical.

I'm not selling vans. The conventional and small economy cars are big enough for most families, but we were ready for a bus.

No claim to wisdom

Sometimes I get the idea that readers expect me to produce words of wisdom. I've been told they benefit from what I say on occasion and that I often show insights into the ways of children.

I think that sometimes children see the world more clearly than do adults, and in many ways I don't think I ever grew up. A child's emotions are close to the surface and I've not been too successful submerging emotion.

In one way or another the joys, fears, frustrations, sorrows, and loves of our lives must be vented. They must find their way to expression. I choose to write, among other things like talk, laugh, cry, scream, and pray.

So, if anyone reads and benefits from my personal therapy—bless you.

I remember parts of my childhood and early adult years rather vividly. Although I'm grateful for all the experiences I've had, I never wished to relive any part of my life. My anticipation of what lies ahead has me far more captivated.

Of necessity, a writer first of all relives experiences in the mind, and then in print.

My children know I wasn't a perfect child. There have been times when I've gritted my teeth when my mother added spice to the plot by telling my children things about me I hoped she had forgotten—or never knew.

With so much nostalgia in the air it would be tempting to long for the good old days. If we can distort the past sufficiently they *can* become the "good old days."

The growing up years had their particular set of joys and sorrows. I pity people who haven't had a generous sprinkling of both. How else do we grow?

Whatever else I might say about my life, I must frankly admit that it has been full of interesting and memorable experiences.

*   *   *

We have five little white puppies at our house. Yes, again! Our dog is a paramour. Lately, she has such a great appetite that she ate one of the kids' lunches before they left for school one morning. It was the last chicken leg, too.

The day chivalry died

When I was eight months and three weeks pregnant with my eighth child I made a routine trip to the grocery store.

I started toward the "IN" door of the market and a middle-aged man was making his exit. It looked as though one of us was going to have to move over to make room for the other, so I stepped a bit to the right.

In stepping to the right I stepped right off a little curb and fell down, spilling the contents of my purse.

I'm not one to look for special favors or handling, but I was so obviously pregnant that I expected some assistance. The man, carrying his bag of groceries, glanced down at me and continued on his way without a word. I put the things back into my purse and tried to get up off the pavement with as much ladylike dignity as possible.

Another man came across the parking lot about that time and I remarked, "I sure am getting clumsy lately." He said that he could sure sympathize with me because he had a lot of trouble like that himself of late. We laughed about it, but I still had to get up under my own steam.

Ordinarily, people have treated me with courtesy. Men and women often have come to my aid when I've run into some inhibiting situations. This was probably an isolated incident.

After my shopping was finished and I was once more behind the steering wheel of my car I stopped to think—something wasn't right. Who killed chivalry?

Environmental/Earth Day

The kids came home all excited about celebrating E-Day (that's for earth or environmental). I suggested they start their observance by cleaning their rooms and the back yard.

The idea didn't appeal to them as much as picking up paper on the school playground, and getting out of a little classroom activity. One look under their beds and in their closets and you can get a pretty good idea what the experts mean by litter.

I'm waiting patiently for the kids to accept my suggestion for noise pollution control as well. I suggest a couple of hours without radios, televisions, banging the front door, and fighting—each day. So far no luck.

*   *   *

Five-year-old Paul was willing to get his hair cut, but wanted to go somewhere besides the barber school.

When I drove up in front of the school he screamed, "NO!"

"Oh, come on now, Paul," said I. Hoping not to be foiled again.

One of the students was standing in the window of the school smiling as I opened the rear door of the car and Paul took a dive over the seat to the back of the station wagon. Another barber joined the first and they smiled.

I lowered the back window and Paul took another dive into the back seat. Another barber joined the first two and they all stood at the window, smiling.

I tried bribery, promising candy or gum if he would walk into the barbershop. He refused. I became frustrated. I gave up and started to roll up the back window and said, "Okay, you win, let's go home so you can take your nap."

I said the magic word—nap. He didn't want to take a nap more than he didn't want to get his hair cut.

"Okay, if you're too big for a nap then you're big enough to walk in there by yourself and get into the barber chair." He did.

I won. When he walked peacefully in the door the barber students applauded and asked, "How did you do it, lady?"

Sometimes mothers are just too battle weary to enjoy victory.

Open letter to a hitchhiker

Dear friend of the road:

I passed you on the road today. It gave me a funny feeling inside. A feeling I quite often get when I pass you by. Me, with this big empty car.

Then your eyes and your thumb follow me in my rear view mirror. I begin to wonder if my judgment was correct.

Sometimes I'll pick you up if you look like a student on the way to class and you might be late if I don't. Once you were a young girl holding a baby under a heavy shawl on a cold, windy day, when all the other cars were passing you by. Once you had trouble with your car and I drove you to the nearest phone, and another time you were out of gas.

I have walked a lot but never hitchhiked. So I don't really know what it's like to stand out there and watch people like me ignore you.

I wish we could be sure that each of you may be as courteous and wholesome as the others we have picked up along the way. In spite of all the terrible things we read in the newspaper we still like to think that people are basically good, and that no harm will come to us if you get into our cars. We would like to share our travels with you. We would like to hear what you have to say about life. We aren't really that indifferent.

It isn't only the driver who is in potential danger. Often it's the hitchhiker who runs into trouble. Young girls who take to the highways with packs on their backs and destination unknown are especially vulnerable.

Quite frankly, I would worry if any of my girls were hitchhiking. It's frightening to read about girls who have been picked up, sexually assaulted, abused—and too often disappear.

So, if I pass you by on the road, please try to understand that I would like to help you out, but there is still that healthy kind of fear that prevents it. It's like learning to swim and not going too far, too deep, or alone in unfamiliar water.

*   *   *

My first-grader came home from school with his first book of paintings. The book had a lovely wallpaper cover. Each painting had its corresponding interpretation written for him by his teacher. The last page in the book had no painting, only a note in the corner, "Picture thrown away because he was painting another boy instead of his picture."

I plan to have a little talk with that boy. This isn't what is meant by "painting people."

What is a human being

A = singular, as in individual.

Human = intellectually and morally superior to other animals.

Being = a state of existence.

There must be a certain something about the human being that tells him life can be better than it is. Some hint of the possibilities that exist. Rather than being a creature of inertia, man is in a state of constant change.

The human mind is active—constantly evaluating, calculating, putting thoughts together, and moving in one direction or another.

Some motivational would-be political psychologists may believe the masses of people should be moving their thoughts and mental development in certain directions, and at specific times. Messages, through print and electronic media, are coming from people who consistently try to motivate great numbers of people.

Those who do not agree with a particular point of view, and are not moved in a particular direction, are not inert. They are active in their own, individual way. To do nothing is action.

Silence, resistance, and sleep have elements of mental decision making and mental activity involvement. We've become intolerant people. Too many activists think everyone should be in perpetual motion for their particular cause.

Few people realize the scope or impact of their demands on individuals and on society. They haven't thought through the possible consequences of their actions. They haven't considered alternatives to their means of achieving the end results.

There are too many publicity hungry people trying to sway the "mass mind" of large and small communities.

The individual human being must sort and cope.

Alienation

The philosopher, Kierkegaard, believed that man's image of self could only be preserved by identifying with God. He called despair over loss of self a "sickness unto death."

Alienation and despair are luxuries that I personally can no longer afford. I've had many doom and gloom moments and, like everyone else felt I'd earned the right of holding on to my feelings. Hope tells us to defy logic if we have to in order to remain in possession of self.

Most of what we read tells us society is grossly corrupt. Perhaps, like the Greeks, we can moan that "Even the gods have deserted us."

It takes a blind faith to continue to identify with God, and maintain self, when darkness surrounds us. There appears to be a glint of light at the end of the long tunnel. Enough to draw us forward.

Meanwhile, we can weep and wail—or lessen the burden of others along the way.

Dehumanization

Our culture has the unique quality of obliterating human beings by saying they do not exist.

The unborn, the infirm, the senile aged are obvious choices for dehumanization because they can't fight back. The young, intelligent and healthy may fight back, but in the fight they lower themselves to a dehumanizing level and become part of the problem.

Most people engage in selective recognition. We pass by people daily, whom we refuse to recognize as existing within our small worlds. A glance up, rather than down, gives at least token recognition. And, it is just as easy to ignore people we know and love as it is to ignore strangers.

There is a constant reaching out of people for people, but very little touching, very little real contact—not just in the physical sense of the word.

Dehumanization is when a person sees others as objects rather than persons, as less than himself.

Concentration camps were possible in Germany because there were enough people willing to dehumanize others, and to dehumanize themselves in the process.

My mountains are molehills

I'm often lonely, but never abandoned.

Though near despair threatens, I cannot yield. Should I waste the years of hard climbing only to look back with doubt and say my hour of need was not aided?

The individual is incapable of compassion until he has experienced the passion (suffering or joy of living).

When the mountains of worry, insecurity, hunger, poverty, false accusations, contempt, disillusionment, frustration and mental-physical incapacity have somehow been reduced to molehills, we have to understand that others are still climbing their mountains. And, another mountain still awaits our climb, and beckons and challenges us to give additional proof that we are all that we claim to be.

I can't bear another person's burden in a crowd. The helping comes more subtly. It's the day-to-day little thoughts, words, and actions that add up. They give me no real sense of righteousness, nothing specific that I can point to with pride and say, "Look, what a great humanitarian I am."

Some can go out and find mountains to climb and wave their flag when they reach the top. But then, mountains have a way of finding me, and I content myself with surmounting molehill after molehill—without flag waving.

Consummation of the world

Man consumes a hearty meal, consummates a marriage, continues to consume material and natural resources, and in the end may suffer and die from a classical case of over consumption.

If man continues to glut away at the expense of all those who own the world, then the world can't help but retaliate. Individuals seem to have lost their sense of justifiable limitations. It would be simple to blame glut consumption on glut availability, but we're assuming a relationship and wisdom in selection of number and kind.

The average American consumer hasn't had to say no (nor has he wanted to) to himself for many decades. Advocating self-control and saying no to oneself is bordering the heretical.

Each individual has his or her excesses and passions and binges. It takes much understanding to accept those excesses in others— along with each person's areas of conservation.

*   *   *

What do you do when you have a nine-month-old baby girl who spits her baby food back in your face? This same little girl prefers eating the dog food by the handful and finishes up by washing her hands in the dog's water bowl.

*   *   *

Five-year-old Paul loves wood, hammer and nails. Last week, he built himself an airplane. I drew the line when he asked for matches to light the tail, as he sat there with his little sister, waiting to take off in his jet.

Possessive pronouns for people

The longer I'm around, and surrounded by, young people, the greater my awareness of my incompetence. I've written about my children because they are a ready and available source of copy.

I have read columns by women whom, I believe, invaded the privacy of their families. I've tried to avoid the type of humor that picks away at the dignity of others, especially family. A column that deals in family relations and personal opinion must also be an exercise in diplomacy and tact.

I write my own observations and not a consensus of my husband's and my opinions. Most often I use singular pronouns. If I use possessive pronouns in describing my relationship to my children it is only to distinguish them from the neighbors' children.

In no way do we possess our children.

We have an obligation to guide their growth, but no right to assume the position of their ruler, owner, or controller. Sometimes there's a fine dividing line.

We may have characteristics that identify us very closely with our parents, but none of us are just like them, or anyone else. No person is just like any other in all departments. The beauty of this human race is that all people are different, and not stamped out like a bunch of blobs.

II

EQUAL TIME FOR ALL

Rational human beings long ago decided to divide our days and nights into an orderly system of time slots. Our personal allotment of time is, in turn, distributed according to priorities. Thus, putting demand on us to organize the use of our time and become productive. At times we feel no rush to meet life's goals—and then, a sense of loss of time overwhelms us and we move with unnecessary haste. Each moment is a gift, and the time comes for us all when we can no longer beg, borrow or steal any more of those precious moments. What, then?

Daily routines set mental clocks

We tell time by the light of day and the dark of night. Usually, with a clock. Little children look at the digital numbers on a clock and get the time of day, long before they have mastered the mechanics of reading hands pointing to numbers. Occasionally we set our mental clocks by the routine of others.

Without looking at a clock, I know there is an order for dismissal at our house on school mornings. There are three buses to catch and three cars to dispatch, with many clues between to indicate when someone is running late. By habit, certain movements follow one right after another, and one person depends on another to be at a certain point in their preparation for the day's labor.

Some eat while others get dressed, and it takes master planning to divide ten people into three bathrooms without major conflict. Fights take extra time.

I've learned to tell the difference between the garbage truck with screeching brakes, school buses that sound smaller and kind of glide to a stop, the neighbors' cars, a train whistle in the distance, clock radios going off, and the front door opening and closing. In the back of my mind I associate each of these sounds with where someone should be at that time.

How many people wake to the sound of the morning newspaper hitting the front door? The sound of a neighbor's car warming up in his driveway? The German Shepherd in someone's back yard stretching its legs and vocal chords?

When I was growing up my father did a lot of running, long before jogging became a sport. He worked the night shift at the bakery and ran home from the bus stop each morning. It wasn't until he changed from the night to the day shift that he found people along his running path had been setting their mental clocks by his routine.

How often does a homemaker gauge her or his housework by the mail delivery, hunger, or a certain television program? Time for a break. We hear a neighbor's car go by in the morning and the first bus catcher had better be on his way. We're on time for work when we turn a corner and see a bakery delivery truck heading toward the hamburger place to drop off the day's supply of buns. The man with his brief case is still on the corner waiting for his car pool ride. The jogger is heading our way. The attendant is changing prices on the sign at the gas station.

Church bells chime and we examine our watches to verify our noontime hunger pangs. The train whistle blows in the distance, and lets us know how much time we have to beat it to the crossing. The factory whistle blows and we know we're late.

Strangers, passing in the night and in the day, never realizing they aid the others journey. What simple faith we have when we depend on the routine of another. What simple trust we have in human beings to be where they are supposed to be, to do their job, make their deliveries, blow their whistles—and set their clocks.

Time management

Nothing aggravates a woman as much as having a man try to tell her how to get her housework organized and run the place like a factory.

Of course, she has a system, and it works well enough for her. But, if this same gal complains about not having enough time to do some of the fun things she'd like to do then she'll get no sympathy from me until she reorganizes and prioritizes her time.

Every homemaker finds him or herself in situations that have certain commitments, priorities and limitations. The best thing I can say about housework is that it has to be done, someone has to do it, and let's get it over with as quickly as possible so we can enjoy life.

It's not that I hate housework, it's just that I can think of hundreds of other things I'd rather be doing.

At some point in her life, a woman decides whether she's going to live in House Beautiful, House Comfortable, or House Messy. A slow reflective inventory walk through the house will give a person the benchmark for deciding, how clean is clean? How much is necessary, desirable, or important.

Then she has to take into consideration the attitude of the rest of the family. How much do they care? If they care a lot and it's rewarding to everyone concerned, then maybe a really clean house should take priority—and they should help. Maybe it's worth the number of hours invested.

What? You say you have no idea how many hours you devote to housework? Maybe a little time and motion study would help.

Follow yourself around for a week. How? Well, mentally. Make a conscious effort to understand what you're doing and why. Use a pencil and paper. Make a diagram of the house and examine your patterns of walking and working. Some women clean from one end to the other once a week. Others clean one room thoroughly on set days. I can't tell you what will work best for you. My system is quite simple—based primarily on necessity. A maid would be nice.

When I had one child I spent more time cleaning house than when I had all eight children at home. Some people will say it looks it, too. But, others have remarked about how good the house looks for the number of people coming and going. Fortunately, I've been able to divide some of the work load by sharing this wonderful experience with my children.

Time is all we have to work with. Many years ago I arrived at a realistic conclusion that I would not have House Beautiful. If you drop by unexpected you may see a child's tennis shoe in the middle of the living room carpet, or yesterday's newspaper beside the easy chair.

So, there might be time for Friday morning bowling, tennis or golf. Time to take a class in conversational Spanish. Time to work with the Girl Scouts or the Boy Scouts. If you already combine full-time home making with a full-time job then you've probably been forced to make time and motion studies to work out a system of getting the job done. On the other hand, you may have figured that you have earned the right to pay someone to come in and give a helping hand with household chores and yard care.

*   *   *

We have an 11-year-old frog lover. She wanted to keep the frogs in her bedroom but we compromised and put them on the sun deck. I've had to leave the light burning on the deck at night so the frogs would think it was daytime and shut up.

Goal setting

If you don't know where you want to go then you won't know when you've arrived.

When I was in my late twenties with three young children, a house to care for, a husband working full-time and going to college part-time, I experienced poor health and mental atrophy.

I made a decision to return to college and set my goal toward a degree. About fourteen years later I reached the goal and was graduated with honors from a four-year university. That's what you call a long-range goal. It wasn't a firm goal because it lacked a time limit.

I probably could have done it much sooner if it had been higher on my priority list. I would have made a more realistic working plan. Only when my youngest child reached age two did I sit down and make a firm plan. I would take all the courses I could at a two-year college and transfer my credits to a four-year university. My plan had to be extended an additional year while I got my tuition together. That's when planning came into the picture.

Reaching my goal required financial planning as well as time management. I didn't want to reach my goal at the expense and neglect of my home and family—and that was a priority.

To reach my long-range goal I had to set short-term goals. Each day had its list of deeds to be done. About the time I had trouble sleeping nights because I was worrying about all the things I had to do the next day I devised my method of list making. Before I went to bed I listed all the jobs to be done the next day, people I had to call on the phone and see, errands I had to run in the car, important activities for the family, and whatever reading or studying I had to schedule.

Most of it got done most of the time.

There was a sense of accomplishment each time I ran a line through a completed task on my list. I used lists for years before I found out how to really make them work for me. Check lists for everything from getting a kid ready for camp to shopping for groceries.

And what happens when you reach your long-range goal? You will have already set another goal and be working toward it. Most likely the new goal is related to the one just reached. When I was six months away from receiving my two-year college degree I was already taking classes at the four-year university and my application for admission was being processed. When I was six months away from receiving my undergraduate degree, my application for admission to graduate school was already in the works. Advance planning got me a teaching assistantship and financing for my advanced degree in communications.

Every plan includes two or three options. If one plan doesn't work out the way it looked on paper then there is little time for disappointment because I pull out option number two, and it may prove the best of the bunch.

Major corporations spend millions of dollars to research and develop ways of reaching their goals. There are hundreds of helpful books written by experts and near experts on the subject of time management and goal setting. No reason why some of these techniques can't be used just as effectively in household management and creating additional, needed time slots.

*   *   *

After years of struggling to get my fingernails to grow, I discovered the secret. Keep them out of water. Don't do any housework. They grow best when I'm confined to a hospital bed. I'll have to compromise, and settle for picking up dimes with my teeth or a bit of chewing gum.

Reward system

Self-motivation is difficult without some kind of reward system. Maybe goodness is its own reward, but a new pair of earrings, lunch at the golden arches, a long-distance phone call to a friend, reading a novel, or an opera ticket can be added incentive.

I took a sack lunch to school for four months. As a reward for all the money I saved I took myself out to lunch three times in three weeks. Most people think they're entitled to go out to lunch any time they're hungry. If I did that I would have to look for another reward system.

The reward system only works if you're willing to forego some immediate satisfaction. Without a little sacrifice it means nothing.

Once or twice a week I let myself watch a movie on television. I look through the weekly programming on Sunday and decide which programs I really want to see. Most people feel they are entitled to watch four hours of television every night and six or eight hours on weekend days. If I did that, then I would have to find another reward system for all the time I force myself to sit down at the typewriter or take out a textbook.

When I get a paycheck I set something aside as reward money. Why, not? It's for a worthy cause.

*   *   *

We had a goldfish named George. He moved marbles around in the bottom of his bowl. Sometimes when the house was very quiet, George became very noisy.

George was the lonely survivor from a group of three goldfish that the children brought home from a store opening. We learned how not to set the goldfish bowl on the windowsill at night because the temperature drops. That's how George lost his roommates.

George received tender loving care but in his loneliness he took up the sport of moving marbles with his nose. I first noticed this phenomenon when I was talking on the phone one day and saw George's tail fins wiggling frantically as he struggled to free a marble with his nose.

At night, when I was in bed, I could hear the marbles moving in the bowl in the kitchen. We never knew for certain if George was male or female—but, I suppose if you're alone in a fish bowl with a bunch of marbles it doesn't really matter.

Thinking time on the road

Hundreds of miles of white line can be hypnotic. The droning of a car radio can put me to sleep. To stay awake I chew gum and play mental games, or listen to talk shows. Time passes more quickly and more productively.

I play an observation game where I pick out the familiar, unfamiliar and unusual landmarks. If I were drawing a map, what kinds of markings would I use so people would know they were following the same trail? When I taught college writing classes, one of the first assignments was for the students to write the directions from their house or work to the school.

As I drive along, I make up stories about the people in the other cars and along the road, those who pull off the road and those who work in businesses along the way. Who lives in the houses by the side of the highway and on the hillsides?

For those who can't play mental games and still concentrate on driving—then, by all means, driving comes first. Games are for skilled drivers who have developed sufficient instinct. There is a mechanism inside us that always alerts itself to the unexpected—some kind of reactor for defensive driving.

Constructive thinking can keep you mentally alert and leave you with a sense of accomplishment at the end of the trip. You can solve business problems, map out sales campaigns, outline a book, analyze a bit of poetry or think through some personal problems.

Try doing characterizations of friends and family members. Determine positive personality traits and identify physical characteristics. What is it that attracts you to certain people? Where did you first meet? These may seem like unnecessary bits of information, but it could strengthen a friendship through better understanding, and improve your mental ability as well.

We get to know people better by being with them and mentally going over the experience later.

Compose a letter to your congressman, the editor of your local newspaper, your parents, or your children, or God. Make resolutions for future action.

Sometimes a tape recorder is a good companion on a trip. Or a notebook to jot down a few words at the traffic light or rest stop. The important thing is not to be overly concerned about what you should remember. Chances are you'll remember the important things. Constructive thinking processes and appreciating being alone in your own mind for a while are profitable time consumers.

Cellular, mobile car phones should be reserved for emergencies, or to be used while the car is stopped and out of traffic. Talking on a phone while driving can be hazardous to your health, and the health of those around you. Some cities and states are banning the use of these phones while driving.

A few words on sticky-note attached to the dashboard can trigger chain reaction thoughts. Keep it simple and keep an eye on the road.

Amateur philosophers play the "why" game. No one is going to pass judgment on your conclusions, so feel free to explore the universe. Why are some things the way they are and not another way? Can life be different? Is there life on other planets? What is my purpose for being?

And the "what" game. What about home improvement? What kind thing can I do for someone who has been good to me? What about self-improvement projects?

Upon reaching a destination, clear the decks by writing down a few thoughts, call home to let those who care know you arrived safely, or just appreciate having spent time getting inside your own head, and getting to know yourself better.

*   *   *

A wife knows she is a success when her husband sleeps while she drives.

Little Miss Two going on three

Life is wondrous, miraculous, monstrous, marvelous, phenomenal, stupendous and fearful when you're almost three years old. Days can be frustrating when the giant people around you don't understand your questions or answers—and your favorite word is "What?" or "What's that?"

Tina is a healthy, active, red-haired little ball of fire who takes advantage of her position as end-of-the-line baby in our household. Sometimes she takes her frustrations out on the rest of us.

She's lovable, laughable, and at least once a day loud and screaming.

She led me a merry chase through the park. She was irritated by the sand in her bathing suit and decided to go naked. She delighted in watching people laugh as she romped and I chased. At one point she decided to climb into the drinking fountain basin and wash her feet.

At times she acts quite grown up. Like the day she walked proudly across the street carrying a gift to her first birthday party.

The other children ask why she repeats everything they say to her. They forgot they did the same. Learning the language is no easy matter and involves repeating and getting feedback. She's beginning to enjoy the sound of her own voice and the novelty of putting words together.

When she isn't repeating she's asking, "What's that?" How better to learn, and unfortunately, annoy. I have to change the answer three or four times before she's satisfied that she understands. We sometimes forget she lives in a rapidly expanding world of new information.

There are times I try to filter out the voices of the other children and her little droning voice doesn't get through until she screams.

We put her back to bed two or three times at night. She's reluctant to let go of her day. Once we thought she was asleep and discovered she was busy emptying her sister's dresser drawers. Another time she fell asleep on top a pile of stuffed animals (like E.T.) on the floor, rather than in her bed.

Life would be dull without her. She helps build up my tensions, and also to relax them. Giving a little girl a big hug is still good therapy for this mother.

Sometimes I hurt inside and don't know exactly why. She doesn't mind if I hold her on my lap for a few moments, maybe shed a few tears and have her wipe them away with her little hand, and most often the hurt feeling goes away.

*   *   *

My husband bought me a gold heart-shaped box of chocolates for Valentine's Day. Tina thought it was hers. She had the wrapper off and gulped down the first pieces of candy before she would let go of the box. I made critical judgments of parents in the past for allowing such behavior. But I know what it's like to be outsmarted by a two-year-old. There are times when you have to impress them with your size and authority.

Life on wheels

A drive-in used to be a place where you sat in the car and watched a movie (or pretended to watch a movie) and a place where you went for a hamburger and a malted milk shake.

Now we have drive-in cleaners, dairies, banks, mailboxes, zoos, car washes, and churches. I heard they've even tried a drive-in funeral parlor. Drive by viewing.

In years to come we'll probably see an increase of drive-in types of businesses; anything to speed the consumer on his way to the next purchase.

It was a great day for me when they opened the drive-in banking service window. I've learned the hard way that you should never leave a child unattended in a car. Once I made a quick trip into the bank and came out to find my car rolled back against a fence, with a police officer standing at the front window talking to a very confused little child. I won't mention any names.

Children love emergency brakes. Especially when the car is parked on a hill. They love to pull the handle and make the car go.

We give them cars to play with before they can walk. Cars are toys, and it takes some of them a long time to get the point of what driving is all about. One of my kids even had a car seat with a steering wheel to help Mummy drive.

The first time my Mother let me drive, I thought I knew it all and it would be great fun. I had a heavy foot and made my first and last sharp turn around the corner. I knew how to make the thing go but hadn't listened to the instructions about how to slow the vehicle down.

Sometimes one mistake is all you get. I insisted the only way I would learn to drive was to get behind the wheel and get the experience. (No driving classes in Catholic school then.) I didn't get my hands on the family car again, except to wash it—until I was married, had two children, and was living in California. I went back to Michigan on vacation, and my parents finally let me drive their car.

My children believe driving is their birthright. They believe you automatically get a permit at fifteen and a license at sweet sixteen. Some should and some shouldn't. For some it's a necessity and for others it's still a toy. They think it's still speedy hot-wheels they're playing with.

Someone should design a game for very young children that will teach them the fundamentals of road courtesy and safety, instead of computer games where you run into each other and race to the finish line.

Cars can become weapons in the hands of irresponsible adults or young people. Insurance companies make a business of protecting us from this weapon. Accident statistics cause them to increase rates for young drivers.

Cars give people a sense of freedom and power. Some offensive drivers would sooner run you off the road as let you fill a space between them and the car ahead. They're in a big hurry. They own the car but not the road.

TV decreases family communication

A crisis is when the large screen television goes on the blink and everyone has to watch his favorite show on a smaller screen.

I don't recall whether my brother and I fought over the family radio to hear our programs, but we probably did on occasion. Choices were somewhat limited. Now, radio is mostly limited to the automobile, head sets and boom boxes. Today, we have hundreds of choices on cable or satellite television.

When my kids hear that we didn't have a television set until I was in high school they think of me as a character from the *Flintstones*. As a matter of fact, I enjoyed radio as much as they enjoy television.

I remember racing home from school to hear the latest episode of *Captain Midnight*, and see if my decoder ring had arrived in the mail. *Jack Armstrong*, *The All American Boy*, *Tom Mix*, and *Fibber McGee* filled imagination time—and the *Lone Ranger* and his Friendly Indian Companion Tonto, kept me on the edge of my seat.

Sunday nights we finished our homework and settled down for the thrillers—*The Shadow* knows, with his chilling laugh, and *Inner Sanctum*, with its creaking door. We listened to the thrillers and chillers in a dark room because they told us to "turn out the lights, turn them out!" So, we did.

My kids have their Saturday morning cartoons on television. My favorite Saturday morning show was *Let's Pretend*. It was exciting to visualize what was happening to the princess and her magic frog, or how the prince went about rescuing his ladylove. *Grimm's Fairy Tales* and other stories probably made me a hopeless romantic, but it didn't squelch my creativity and enthusiasm for reading.

I couldn't believe *Uncle Milty* and the now discredited *Soupy Sales* would ever replace *One Man's Family* or the *Lux Movie Theater*— but they did.

My mother had just as much trouble pulling me away from the radio or a good book as I do getting my children away from the television on Saturday morning, when there are chores waiting. Sometimes I think they leave the TV going in an empty room because they think the room will get lonesome, or the TV will never start again.

I couldn't get excited about the fact that there would be a new Saturday morning cartoon added to the already abundant list. There was a time when I could plan getting everyone moving by 11 a.m., but the common refrain is "just 'til we see the end of this one." And, if I'm not watching, another one starts before I know it.

In moments of desperation I've turned off, unplugged, and removed a television from the center of childish attention. I have a long-standing battle with TV consuming the lives of my children. Even when we go on vacations, at the beach or in the mountains, there's a conveniently placed television set in the center of activity. And it usually goes on before we get the car unpacked.

I love to watch television. I strenuously object to its excessive use. I enjoy settling down and watching one program all the way through without having to jump up to attend to some other matter. Those occasions are rare, maybe that's why I'm not addicted to TV—and maybe that's why I'm envious of the kids having nothing else to do.

TV is here to stay, along with other amazing advances in technology. I will adjust to its intrusion into most of the waking and some of the sleeping hours of the day. It would be difficult to live without it after becoming accustomed to its friendly voices. It gives us all a means of escape, and a steady flow of all sorts of news. Something to hide in front of to avoid confrontation and communication with real live people.

Television has become the great American way of passing time. When people are young and lonesome, or old and lonesome, it's easier to set them in front of the moving picture than to be there in person to keep them company. It has become the national babysitter or caretaker for young and old alike.

Can we look forward to effective family communication if everyone is staring straight ahead and saying, "Don't bother me now I'm busy watching a program. It's almost over." Most people won't recognize this behavior as a put-down or a shut-out of others.

There are times when I feel like throwing the main switch on every TV in America to see what would happen. Probably the live fight-of-the-week would take place in most homes.

No home should be without means of communication with the outside world, but like everything else it requires some control of use. I know I'm different. Too much TV makes Marilyn a dull girl. There are things to do. Read books and talk with people.

Now, computers, hand-held games, Internet and chat rooms— there's a whole new and different way to avoid talking with real people face to face.

Staying awake at the circus

I took four young children to the circus one Saturday afternoon. I didn't want to take them at night when they would be tired and fall asleep.

When the lights were lowered and the acts began, I gradually lost interest and alternated closing one eye then the other, drifting into half sleep several times.

The "Great Bruno" was balancing himself on top of a pole that reached to the ceiling of the coliseum. The last words I heard before I drifted off again were "You'll see him bend to the breaking point!"

I awoke suddenly to the view of Bruno appearing to fall from his high perch. I jumped up and screamed, "Oh my God!" and the kids started to laugh.

"Were you really scared?" they asked, and delighted in having the joke on me.

I wouldn't have fallen asleep at the first circus I attended. When I was a very young lady, a very young man escorted me to my first big circus. Autograph books were quite popular then, and the young man proved his affection for me by getting signatures from most of the circus performers. I think he got everyone but the elephants. He probably would have tried but I told him the book was full.

Like many of our memories, that treasured book with the smallest man in the world's autograph has disappeared.

When the military draft was a thorn

There was a time when I was in favor of the National Lottery draft system—but that seems long ago when it was a carryover from the emergency effort of World War II. And, before I had sons.

In projecting ahead, I went down the lists of numbers drawn one day in the lottery. If my two sons were old enough they would have been numbers 281 and 293. They would have been among the fortunate ones near the end of the line who could breathe a bit easier and plan their future with a feeling of some doubtful security.

It's easy to speak of the nobility of fighting for just causes when your sons are little, or when you have no sons. But when a son nears 18 the whole issue of the draft becomes pressing. I find my enthusiasm for "just causes" diminishing with their increasing age.

I'm in sympathy with the people of Vietnam, faced with threats to their lives if we suddenly withdraw support. I'm also in sympathy with the agony of other peoples who have been driven from their homes and oppressed. The people of Hungary, Poland, East Berlin, Palestine, Native Americans, and Africans—and all the other places and people who have been denied the basic liberties of life that we enjoy.

How much can we do, and how far can we go as a nation? Are there no limits to what the world expects from America in the way of finances, arms and military personnel?

We've made some progress in helping people to help themselves, but then again we have interfered in many countries, supported dictatorships, and brought about an anti-American climate.

For a long time we dealt ineffectively with the force of communist aggression. Our foreign policy was pragmatic and unclear. We avoided a world war and hung around long enough for the Soviet Republic to collapse and dismantle itself, and see the Berlin Wall come tumbling down.

In a situation where we have an undeclared war effort it is still doubtful whether we, as a nation, have the right to call young men or women to serve. In the absence of a national emergency it is doubtful, at least in my mind, whether we have a right to ask our men and women to bear arms and serve on foreign soil.

There will always be unresolved questions that the powers that be in Washington debate while our sons grow older, or die.

I tried very hard to believe that our involvement in Vietnam was the right thing to do. Nothing appears quite so simple as a situation viewed from the outside. And, as I rewrite this column, we are poised to attack Iraq—because we intend to disarm their leader. If I do another rewrite in another few years we will be on the verge of a conflict somewhere in the world, if a world still exists.

I've long supported the idea of a volunteer military force. Now we have one, and my youngest son joined the Navy and served fourteen years. He wasn't engaged in battle, but he joined and served because it was his choice. There will always be men and women who choose to serve, and they are better for it. It is an honorable profession. They will always be there, to come to the aid of their country—for within this country resides their families, their freedom, their fortunes, great or small.

If a man's nobility and sense of righting a wrong extends beyond the limits of his own country then I feel sure there will be ways for him to reach out and aid his brothers elsewhere in this vast world of suffering. Whether through military or humanitarian efforts, hopefully the job will get done.

Although the military draft and the Vietnam effort are past history, I fear that the people of this nation forget rather quickly that the world is far from solutions to peaceful coexistence. For centuries other mothers have felt as I did when I wrote most of the above. History has a vicious way of repeating itself, because we learn so little from the past.

A dog's day in court

Every man or woman is entitled to his or her day in court—even when his or her dog runs afoul of the law.

It didn't make much of an impression on our little white poodle when I scolded her for wandering across the street in front of the dog control vehicle. It did make quite an impression on the kids when I told them I was going to court because "their dog" got a ticket.

"Please don't go to court! Please pay the fine!" they begged. But I refused to listen. I'd never been to court before, and thought it would be interesting. I worked for an attorney at one time and delivered documents to the courthouse, but never watched him in action. Perry Mason was my hero, and I wanted some first hand experience in a courtroom. Even though it was just a dog citation.

The kids associated going to court with going to jail. They've been watching a lot of Perry Mason on television as well. Granted, it would have been much simpler to write a check and drop it into the mail. That's what most normal people do when they get a traffic ticket or a dog violation citation.

I tried to talk myself out of my nervousness. I allowed plenty of time to drive to the courthouse and find a parking place. I didn't want to get a traffic ticket on the way.

The courtroom felt unfriendly, waiting for the judge to appear. We had plenty of time to think. I looked at the others in the room and wondered what they were doing there, and supposed they were wondering about me as well. No one talked.

Three men accompanied by police officers were already in court custody and their business was taken care of first. When they left, along with their friends, families, and attorneys the courtroom was nearly empty.

One woman was called forward on dog control business. Then the judge said an attorney had been unable to appear in court on his dog-at-large citation because he had to be in another court on client business. I figured dog-running-loose charges could happen to anyone—even an attorney or a judge.

Then I was called. I was uncomfortable in spite of the fact that the judge made every effort to put me at ease. I didn't say any of the things I'd planned. I was informed that I could have had a jury trial or another hearing had I chosen to plead not guilty, but all I could see was the children pleading with me not to go to court. So, I did what any good citizen would have done under the circumstances, I pleaded guilty on behalf of my dog. If I'd mailed in the check I would have been doing the same thing. But, standing before a judge and saying you're guilty is a whole different ball game. It's humiliating.

The judge read me the law and gave me a warning for the future, and reduced the fine.

A bad case of the hurriups and worriovers

"Hurry up and wait! Hurry up and wait!"

Men in military service know the feeling. Now, it appears that we're all infected with the hurriups.

Walter works at the corner gas station. He pumps gas into my car (this is Oregon folks) as he speaks hurriedly, telling me about all the customers who come in on their way to or from the freeway.

"It starts with the first customer and it goes on all day. They want service, and they want it right now." He laughed when reminded of the "10-Second Man" servicing a car in a television commercial. "If they'd all get up ten minutes earlier in the morning it would cut down on the hurry for us all.

"I tell them if they can wait long enough I've got an invention I'm working on. When they ask what it is I tell them that when it's perfected I'll be able to see them coming and shoot the gas right into the tank. They won't even have to stop.

"Maybe it's just because I'm getting older," said Walter, "that people seem to be in a bigger hurry," and at that he hurried over to a waiting customer who's front tire was resting on the cord that kept the bell ringing for service.

It isn't just happening at gas stations, it's everywhere. It becomes increasingly evident during holiday seasons. People wind up their motors for a big case of the hurriups and bigger case of the worriovers, and they want everything yesterday.

People with the disease of worriover aren't as easy to identify as those with the hurriups. But, the two usually go together. People with worriovers are greatly concerned with everything—the time of day, the weather, their health, someone else's health, and especially over their severe case of the hurriups. They tell everyone they meet how busy they are and admit it will probably be the death of them yet. But they're so addicted to rushing that they can't seem to take the time to find a cure.

Everyone knows a big dose of slow-m-downs early in the morning with repeated doses every hour is the cure.

Time to say, "Thank You, Mr. Policeman"

"We know that people appreciate what we do but they don't take the time to write or let us know very often," said the police chief. "When we do get a letter of appreciation we make sure the city council is made aware.

The mayor read a letter of appreciation at a city council meeting. The letter mentioned specifically the reduction in traffic problems.

When asked about the traffic situation the police chief said that problems had taken a tremendous drop due to selective enforcement.

Concentration on key trouble spots resulted from contact with members of the community in identifying areas of greatest concern.

"A lot of people contact us personally," said the chief, "they even come in, or stop an officer on the street to give this type of information."

The chief believes his officers are establishing good public relations based on the old "police beat" procedure of placing a man in an area where he becomes thoroughly familiar with the people and places. The police know their beat and the people know them by name.

"Let's not lose our identity," said the chief, "we're not just the 'man in blue' we're human beings and agents of the public."

The police department may receive 10 or 15 letters of appreciation each year for the work they do. They may receive four or five phone calls of thanks each month. At times people on the street will let them know they are appreciated.

The chief said that for the most part they are doing a good job, unnoticed, but his men are "career officers—not just doing a job without thanks."

Sometimes the chief receives complaints on the way an officer handled a case or conducted himself or herself at the scene of an accident. These reports go into the individual officer's personal file and are taken into consideration at promotion time. Letters of appreciation are also posted in the squad room for all to see.

The chief admits they don't get many letters but the ones they do get are cherished. Children write thank you letters when officers make presentations at schools, and there are formal letters of appreciation for narcotics information programs presented to high school students and adult groups.

A spontaneous little thank you note from an eight-year-old read in part, "Thank you for being our police department."

*   *   *

There was a time when the girls wore hand-me-down clothes from their older sisters. Now they get them from their older brothers.

Waiting to die is a lonesome time

The aged and the infirm need love and understanding.

Love can be as simple and effective as a smile or a warm hand reaching out.

Understanding can be taking the time to listen.

Most residents of nursing homes have family and friends who care about them. Sometimes visitors are frequent, but many of them have few callers—and they are far between.

An elderly gentleman dresses in his best suit and tie and sits in the sun on the front porch of the nursing home. His transistor radio is tuned to a talk show to keep him in touch with the issues and with people.

A white-haired lady with a heavily lined face sits in a wheel chair and rubs her hands together. She complains that she doesn't use them much anymore. She used to knit faster than anyone she knew, but now she gets disgusted and quits.

A centenarian claims that "lots of hard work" has kept her looking so well. She survived her children and was brought to the nursing home by her grandson. Three great-grandchildren often come to visit.

Charitable groups take it upon themselves to visit the aging. At one time I belonged to such a group, and we attempted to bring some sunshine into the lives of those who received few visitors.

I visited Joseph once a week for several months. When I entered his room he turned the light on over his bed, donned his sun visor to shade the glare from his eyes, and sat up on the edge of his bed. His feet were gangrenous and always cold. I gently put his slippers on his tender feet and covered his legs with a lap blanket.

Then, Joseph would tell me about his long, good life. He held no resentments or hatreds. He looked forward to death as his last reward for living the kind of life he thought best. In his simple broken English, he told me of his early life in Mexico and of his wonderful wife and children.

The day I went to visit Joseph and his room was dark and his bed empty, I tried not to feel sadness, for I knew he was where he wanted to be. But I still carry a vague memory of him, along with the other important people in my life who have taught me something about dying—and living.

Death—the ultimate thief of time

The older we get the more there is to learn. So much that interests us, and there is a desire to see the world set right.

We keep adding our years—one day at a time, but in the process we accumulate a wealth of knowledge and experience. And so many more opportunities facing us in the future.

We all hope to do something worthwhile with the amount of time we have. Of all the things we have abused and wasted the sting of lost time will continue to cause feelings of regret.

*   *   *

For the person who likes to have the last word in absolutely everything there is a pay now—go later plan available at local funeral directors.

Funeral directors are reluctant to call it a burial insurance policy, and so it comes under many names. It makes sense to do some pre-planning for what may prove to be the most important day of your life. If your family knows you're willing to settle for a pine box rather than keep up with the Jones' by purchasing an expensive casket they can't afford, then they can shake off the guilt feeling when they make your wishes known.

Many of the ethical funeral directors urge people to discuss funeral expenses and arrangements long before the need arises.

One funeral director said, "I come in contact with grief, sorrow and extreme emotional stress almost every day. In some cases much of the resulting confusion and wrongful decisions could be avoided by some form or pre-planning and thinking about what steps must be taken before and after death occurs."

Death creates an emotionally charged atmosphere. The survivors respond and react in a variety of ways with their grief. It's a time when those who are still living seem least capable of mutual support and understanding.

$$* \quad * \quad *$$

Carlos Castaneda spent several years in an anthropological investigation of Don Juan Matus, a Yaqui Indian sorcerer in Sonora, Mexico.

From Castaneda's search into the knowledge and wisdom of Don Juan came several extremely interesting and haunting books. In the *Journey to Ixtlan* Don Juan is trying to help Castaneda understand that death is his constant companion. Castaneda agrees that it may be true but that he prefers not to think about it for it causes him apprehension.

Don Juan explains that thinking about your death doesn't mean worrying about it. "Use it," said Don Juan. "Focus your attention on the link between you and your death, without remorse or sadness or worrying. Focus your attention on the fact you don't have time and let your acts flow accordingly. Let each of your acts be your last battle on earth. Only under those conditions will your acts have their rightful power. Otherwise they will be, for as long as you live, the acts of a timid man."

III

SUCCESS FROM FAILURE

Failure is the primary human condition. More often than not we fall short of our expectations or the expectations of others. Life is totally experimental. What little success we enjoy is the result of having had the guts to try, fail and learn. The frustration comes when we become so wise that we understand and accept the facts of failure and others choose not to learn from our experiences. They insist on learning, as we did, by their own mistakes. That, indeed, is life.

He didn't make a mistake in 4,000 years

What's wrong with being wrong? Senators and congressmen make mistakes. Businessmen and scholars make mistakes. Movie stars make mistake after mistake. Scientists learn by making mistakes. So why should I get shook up if I make a mistake?

What is a mistake? It's a misunderstanding or misconception, a misinterpretation of something someone says or does. When we try our approach and it doesn't work then we admit that our assessment of the situation was erroneous and we try again.

Great things happen because little people make mistakes and learn things from them. The inventor's workroom is full of mistakes. The writer's wastebasket overflows with mistakes. Our lives are full of mistakes. So what? No one tells us to keep making the same mistake over and over again. In fact if we do persist in our mistakes then there *is* something wrong.

By whose interpretation are we mistaken? What may appear

to be a mistaken notion to you might be the verge of discovery to the scientist. Some of our ideas will appear to be crazy to someone else. Even close friends view the same event in slightly different ways.

Many mistakes are costly. Sometimes poor judgment leads to crime, loss of friendships, family, possessions, or freedom. It would be great if such mistakes could be avoided, but when mistaken judgment causes harm to others then the members of a society have a right to expect payment.

Herman Lincoln Wayland, an early American clergyman, said that "the only people who make no mistakes are dead people. I saw a man last week who has not made a mistake in four thousand years. He was a mummy in the Egyptian Department of the British Museum."

I think it's a mistake to try to save our children from making mistakes. Certainly we should give them all the advice and information possible to help them make correct decisions, but they will even tell us if we listen, "Let me learn for myself. Let me make my own mistakes."

There are some who can't learn from the mistakes of others. Some who must touch the fire to prove that it is hot. Obviously we will never experience everything first hand. It would be foolish to try.

Those who observe the actions of others can often make more reasonable judgments than those who are having the experiences.

One advantage of aging is that we do learn more all the time, from our mistakes and the mistakes of others. Why are we so surprised when our youth exercise poor judgment?

Our young people have to contend with a flood of information and advice coming at them from all directions. Life becomes confusing. Mass media communication has provided them with blessings and problems. They have to work harder at selectivity.

We live in a fast moving society of shifting values and it's not only the youth who suffer because of it all.

It's difficult to keep up with the happenings on the international, national and local scene. It's difficult keeping up with what the kids are doing at school and almost tragic trying to arrange schedules and use of the family car. Every week has its conflicts of interest.

More and more we are depending upon others to make our decisions for us. We seek advice from specialists in all fields because we can't possibly cover all the bases.

Children feel the swiftness of time in this space age. When I was growing up there seemed to be plenty of time to burn. Growing up took a long time. Now the kids admit that time is going so fast they are amazed.

In all this hurry and confusion it's understandable that people make errors in judgment. We know so much about communication that it becomes increasingly difficult to communicate on the same levels. The right word at the wrong time "and nobody's perfect" the kids tell me.

The mistake isn't the important thing in our lives—it's what we do after we make a mistake that counts.

*   *   *

I picked Mary up from her kindergarten class and as soon as I closed the car door she blurted out, "Chris kissed me two times when the teacher wasn't looking!"

Very interesting, I thought.

"I don't know why he kissed me?" she puzzled.

"He probably thinks you're a very nice little girl," I said.

"I think he loves me," she said, and wrinkled up her nose as though she'd just bit into a lemon. Then she added, "He told me not to kiss him back or he wouldn't marry me."

After a few moments of silence she volunteered more information. "He told me not to tell my mom or dad."

"Oh really, and why did you tell me then?"

"Because I wanted to."

And, I couldn't remember if I'd told my mother when a boy kissed me for the first time. As my kindergarten friend and I walked home from school he edged me off the sidewalk into the bushes and planted a juicy kiss on my lips. I ran home to wash my mouth out and brush my teeth. I was outraged. Then time taught me it wasn't all that bad after all.

*   *   *

My second grade son invited me to have lunch with him at his school during "National School Lunch Week." I paid, and he surprised me with his good manners. When he was finished with his lunch he took his tray to the window where all good children return their things when they are finished eating. He returned and picked up my tray—and came right back.

"You didn't finish your milk," he said.

"Was I supposed to?" I asked.

"Yes!" he said firmly.

I drank it to the last drop. He was satisfied and I was full.

To receive is blessed, too!

There are times when receiving with true humility and gratitude can be rewarding. Many years ago I had a powerful lesson in how to receive charity from a group of women in our parish.

A group of women provided temporary help when the mother of a family was ill at home, hospitalized, or home with a new baby. They arranged for day care for preschoolers to give the mother an opportunity for rest. Some kind woman would take ironing home and bring it back neatly stacked or on hangers. Others would pool their resources to provide home cooked meals for the family.

The group had one problem. The project was ready to go but we hadn't been able to put it into practice.

A fourth baby was due soon in our household and I considered myself an efficient homemaker. So much so that when one of the women from our parish called and asked if they could provide meals for my family when I came from the hospital and do my ironing I was mildly insulted.

After all, why should I receive charity when there were so many others who needed it far more?

"But, we're just getting started. We need someone to try our program on," pleaded my parish friend. "You'd really be doing us a favor."

"Since you put it that way," I agreed, "I'll be happy to let you use my family for a trial run."

Every good deed or idea needs fertile ground to grow. There was no need for me to be reluctant when offered an act of real charity. We practice our charity on others for most of our lives because we prefer it that way, but we should be willing to let others practice their charity on us.

So much of our existence depends on being open and receptive. Perhaps the people who have cups running over have learned to be good receivers and have an abundance to give.

We receive advice from experts. Help from the strong and the weak. Love from those we love and wish to love. Sympathy and empathy come from anyone willing to listen to our complaints and problems. And great favors coming in strange packages from every source imaginable.

During the early days of Christianity one of the Roman contemporaries of St. Paul, Lucius Annaeus Seneca, a stoic philosopher, said, "We should give as we would receive, cheerfully, quickly, and without hesitation; for there is no grace in a benefit that sticks to the fingers."

*   *   *

Have you removed all the tags on your merchandise that read, "DO NOT REMOVE THIS TAG under penalty of law" or "UNDER PENALTY OF LAW this tag not to be removed?" I see now that some manufactures are adding, "except by the consumer."

I bought an item at a garage sale and the tag was still on, and I chuckled to myself. When I was a kid, putting clean sheets on the beds, I remember seeing those tags sticking out of the mattresses. Someone told me never to remove the tags—so I didn't, though often tempted. How did I know what terrible fate would befall me if I removed a tag that said "do not remove under penalty of law." I didn't know who was patrolling or what the penalty might be, but refused to take chances.

I finally got the message that the tags are for store people, not house people. My own children gleefully rip the tags off along with the wrappings. Fortunately, I've spared them an inhibited childhood.

Personal piano failure
creates concert appreciation

The concert hall lights dim, the auditorium is bathed in darkness, except for the well-lighted stage. Van Cliburn was seated at the piano, poised to begin. You could hear a pin drop. Then, someone who couldn't wait for the first notes to cover for him, coughed. Then, another coughed. Then my throat began to tickle and I reached into my purse for a cough drop.

Cough drops should be standard emergency equipment for the theater buff. Such a habit has saved me many an embarrassment during a quiet moment.

Some theatergoers don't realize that the performance isn't over until the house lights come on again. Those who left the Van Cliburn concert when the last programmed piece was completed missed four encores, including some dynamic Chopin.

I once read a story titled *The Protégé* which delved into the minds of the audience. I wonder how many people go to concerts to be seen rather than to see. Culture, you know! Some poor, hard working husband indulges his wife as an escort, but snores through the low notes.

If you find yourself dozing then supposedly you haven't developed taste for fine music, or asked the person next to you to poke you if you snore. I try mental pictures to accompany the music. Long pieces provide background for an epoch. There are waterfalls, raindrops, sunshine, storms, children at play, and grass growing.

Most of the time the beauty of the music wraps me up in emotion that becomes it's own story, and thoughts are unnecessary.

I appreciate piano talent because I failed. I couldn't arch my fingers. My teacher became disgusted with me and I often went home crying. How sad to have that happen to a pupil who desired so much to learn. I understand that many teachers aren't nearly so determined to take all the fun out of learning. I got the other kind.

Someday, when I'm very brave, I may try again.

Our five-year-old is learning to play piano. Her nine-year-old sister (who never had a lesson) is teaching her. She marks corresponding numbers on the piano keys with black crayon. Mary looks at the numbers in the beginner's book and then at the keys. She has learned to play very short pieces.

Each day when she comes home from kindergarten she goes directly to the piano and plays the same pieces. She's having fun. And when her fingers grow a little longer she may still want lessons. I hope so.

*   *   *

Four-year-old Tina was dawdling about saying night prayers. "Where is God?" she looked around the room.

"He's everywhere," I responded.

"*She's* everywhere!" said my little liberated female.

Farewell to Fritzie

Sometime I wish I could be hard-boiled, cold-blooded, and objective. Today is one of those days.

As soon as five of the children left for school this morning I called the county dog control and explained that our dog, Fritzie, was very ill and getting along in years and would they please come for him.

"Please try to have someone here before the children come home from school," I pleaded.

"We can't say for sure what time it will be," the business-like voice at the other end responded, "but we'll try."

Before I had time to hang up the receiver I was already choking back the lump in my throat. The family will never forgive me. But, they have to. No one else would make the decision, and it had to be made.

I remember when we brought Fritzie home from an Elks' picnic. I was pregnant with Teresa. Teresa is now past seven and I guess Fritzie is really her dog. She has been waiting to take his picture to school all year to show the other kids, and we were able to provide one for her just last week. She was so pleased.

My mind flashes back to a sunny summer day when I was fifteen, and had to take my dog for a long walk on the end of a leash to the dog pound. He barked a lot. My mother was recovering from the miscarriage of my almost sister. The barking dog made my mother nervous.

Tiny, that was the name of my dog, a white Toy Terrier. And I loved him. When I felt lonesome he was there to comfort me, or for me to comfort him. I couldn't stop the tears from flowing the whole mile I walked him to the pound. Hoping he would find a new home. We stopped several times while I sat on a curb and looked into his big round unsuspecting brown eyes. I gave him a hug, dried my eyes and went on. When I handed him over to the man at the counter I was tearful and speechless. The man asked if I wanted to keep the leash. I gulped back gripping emotion and started running for home. I wanted to run so fast that I wouldn't feel the pain—the loss.

Some memories are indelible. And even today, as I wait for the dog control people to come to take Fritzie away, I try to avoid looking at those big brown, woeful eyes. After all, I tell myself, Fritzie does have a heart problem. And who has been giving him his pills twice a day? That's right! I learned how to give my dog, Tiny pills many years ago—before I had to take him for that long walk. No one else in the house has shown the least interest in learning how it's done. They've stood around and watched while I risked a bitten hand.

The poor old Cocker Spaniel is losing his teeth and with those he has left he can't do justice to a good bone. His golden fur, once his pride and joy glistening in the sunlight after a bath, is half gone and he's covered with mange. Fritzie is really a southern California dog, and maybe two winters in Oregon have been too much for him. His coat is too thin to get through another winter.

Nothing I tell the children will be satisfactory. I remember when I was a kid, even before I had my dog Tiny, I cried three quarters of the way through *Lassie Come Home*, and sometimes after when I even thought about the movie. Maybe people like me shouldn't have dogs. Maybe we get too attached. Maybe we're just too "dog-gone" sentimental.

Everybody goes through this sort of thing. But that's no consolation at the moment. When I explain that this was the most humane way it will probably fall on deaf ears when the first person discovers the absence of the family pet.

Fritzie has been a nuisance, granted. Occasionally, we received a Sunday morning phone call telling us to keep our dog quiet. His barking is shrill and has bothered us, too. I can hear him in the backyard now, probably chasing birds. He has also taken nips at visiting neighbor children when they got too near the play pen where he was baby sitting, or too near his bone. I've felt secure with Fritzie as a watchdog in the evening when I'm alone with the children.

Poor Fritzie! It's hard to write a eulogy when you're still out there soaking up the sunshine. I sure hope the man comes early so I don't have to spend the whole day waiting and wondering. Wondering how I'll react when they take him, wondering how I'll face tearful Teresa, and a few other sad faces.

I've already threatened, "No more dogs," but also wonder how long I'll be able to live up to that one.

Oh, no! There's the doorbell!

*   *   *

Career woman: "Who do you work for?"
Housewife: "I'm in a joint partnership."
Career woman: "Fascinating! What kind of a business?"

| Housewife: | "We operate a convalescent home. When my husband is sick and tired of working; I can't stand any more shopping, meetings or part-time work; and the kids are through with school for the day we recuperate in our convalescent home. |

* * *

Career woman:	"And what kind of work do you do?"
Housewife:	"I'm a machine operator."
Career woman:	"How interesting. What kind of a machine?"
Housewife:	"Oh! The washing machine, clothes dryer, vacuum cleaner, dishwasher, sewing machine, microwave and lawnmower.

Noise pollution

"Quiet please!" I shouted.

How can anyone expect to bring silence by adding to the din? I never used to say "shut up" but now I find it slipping out more often.

I read a book about noise pollution and decided that noise beyond a certain point causes me pain. Place seven active children and a crying baby in an unacoustisized kitchen in the heat of the summer with the air conditioner blowing—and that's unorganized sound. My added shouts aid little to calm the waves of noise.

Sound often reaches the point where one person's enjoyment is causing another person a pain in the head. Children seem to be able to stand considerably more noise than their elders. I've tried to talk to my offspring about their noise pollution until I'm hoarse and they turn a deaf ear.

Apparently rock music must be played loud to be enjoyed. I reserve some strong doubts about that. According to some authorities many of our teenagers will grow hard of hearing long before their time as a result of listening to loud electrified music. I've suspected this when I've observed children seeming not to hear when I'm trying to discuss homework or housework.

Older folks with grown children gone from home don't always appreciate the quiet, lonely days and nights without the laughter and screaming of children. I try to remember this when noise pollution levels rise.

Some people like a lot of noise and can't live without it. Then there are those different kinds of people who need quiet to think—to create.

On a bulletin board in a classroom of my youth a teacher pinned up the words "Silence is Golden." I believed it. Only now it's more scarce than gold.

We've become accustomed to using sound to screen out noise. Children study by radio or television to block out household sounds. The hair dryer is a good retreat for thinking. To drown out the sound of my electric typewriter (before I had a computer) I load the washer and dryer in my laundry room office. And, of late I've taken to playing music on the radio to block out the sounds of children fighting in the other rooms.

I'm grateful to be able to enjoy good sounds: the warning sounds, the sound of another person's voice, the sounds of entertainment. I wouldn't want to turn off any of it. But I want to be able to enjoy it longer. So, "Quiet, please!"

*   *   *

As I anxiously perused the teacher's comments on one of my first manuscripts for a creative writing class the air went out of my balloon. She said, "My dear, if your story was written for therapy it probably worked."

*   *   *

I lived in Michigan before I was married. My future husband was stationed at Walker Air Force Base in Roswell, New Mexico. He and four of his buddies were all from the Detroit area. There was one airman who enjoyed spreading rumors that they were "getting out next week." He even had his congressman working on his early release.

While this particular airman was attending a training school in Chicago for a brief period during the two years they were based in Roswell, the others decided to get even. They wrote letters saying how wonderful it was to be out of the Air Force and back in Detroit. They told him it was a shame he missed the early release because he was attending school in Chicago.

My husband-to-be mailed the letters to me and I went along with the gag by dropping them in the mail to get the Detroit postmark.

When the airman in Chicago received the letters from Detroit he hit the ceiling. He went to his commanding officer, and others of influence, insisting that the rest of the guys were out and he was supposed to be released along with them.

The squelch came when the airman's superior in Chicago yielded to persistence and contacted Walker Air Force Base and verified that the group was definitely still in.

The conspiracy guaranteed the Detroit group the remaining six months of rumor-free service once the indignant airman returned to his unit from Chicago.

Profile of a professional drinker

"Warning! The contents of this bottle could be injurious to your wealth."

Don't hold your breath waiting for the official governmental warning on a bottle of booze. It may never come, and if it does it may already be too late for some.

> Have to get courage to make the sale.
> Have to celebrate the big commission.
> Have to drink to forget the failures.
> Have to drink with the boss.
> Have to drink with the other salesmen and coworkers.
> Have to drink with the customers.

And, what about conventions? Have to do double time. Talking with a lot of people and getting dry. Filling the glass more often. On the town with customers, drink for drink. Really hate it, but no way out.

Now drinking becomes a goal in itself. Only associate with customers who like to drink. Unload the others quick. Hang around with the same salesmen after Friday night meetings. It's a challenge to down-'em-double and close the bar.

No time for a social life at home. The wife is capable of taking care of the kids and the house. As long as the money comes in why should she care.

There's a burning sensation in the pit of my stomach in the morning. Breakfast tastes terrible. Grab a cup of coffee and forget the rest. Getting a little edgy with the wife and kids. They get on my nerves. They can't seem to understand that I work hard all week and need my rest. I don't need to hear all their garbage at night when I come home. Start working late, more often. Called at first but gave that up. Couldn't stand the crying and complaining.

Spending more time on the road. Look forward to traveling. No one to bug me about where I should be. A couple of good sales and everyone is happy. No sweat!

Over slept. Damn! Missed the appointment. Used to be able to get up at the crack of dawn. Eyes are blurred in the morning, and hands shake a little. If I drank before noon I'd swear I was an alky like Clarence. You can smell it on him before the coffee break. Disgusting!

What day is it?

How did I get home from the office party last night? I looked in the garage and my car wasn't there. I wonder where it's parked?

My wallet is empty. Damn wife's probably been picking my pocket again. Don't I bring her enough money as it is?

What's this bar bill? Oh, yes! I've been signing the tab. Let's work it into the expense account—a little juggling here and there— no one will know. It's not like stealing or taking it out of the family budget. That would be crude and ungentlemanly.

I can't stand the pain in my gut. Just a little drink will steady my hand and calm my nerves. It's almost noon. An early lunch won't matter. Be all ready for the customer. The big account comes in at one o'clock. I can put in a full day's work in two hours. Not like these young "know nothings."

What's that flashing light in the rear view mirror? Not another cop! They sure have it in for me.

"Just a couple of drinks with the boys, officer. I'm just a few blocks from home. I'm on my way there now. My wife called me to say one of the kids is sick." Now I'll have to go home, he's following me to see that I get there okay.

Got out of that one. They can't pin a DUI (driving under the influence) on me. Can't catch me with a fancy Breathalyzer or balloon test. Next time I'll take a cab.

Income tax returns to file. Where do you claim the business expenses for the bar bills? Let's work them into the socially necessary entertainment expenses. It's all part of the game. Everybody does it.

The income tax return won't be filed jointly next year. I'll have to figure a new way of getting around some of these expenses. Wives don't appreciate what a guy has to do to make a decent living these days. She had her nerve getting a divorce. Said I drank too much. How does she know? She never saw me take a drink. Never drank at home in front of the kids. Really a good guy when you think about it.

Lonely? Who, me?

What's that? The boss said I had to shape up or ship out. The most unsympathetic guy I've ever known. No appreciation for all the business I brought in here. Said my sales have been dipping for months. Sure they are with all the trouble I've had at home.

It's about time people realized they need me. I don't need any of them. I'll show them all how successful I can be without them.

> I'll even stop drinking.
> Why can't I stop?
> I'll just have one to stop the jitters.
> What happened?
> Tomorrow. Tomorrow, I'll quit.
> I ache all over, but I'll quit.
> Right after this one . . .

Some recover alone.
Some recover with help.
Some can't.
Some won't—alone or with help.
Some die slow.
Some die quick.
But, anyone who sincerely desires to recover, can.

Lament of the drinker's family

We live in hope. All of us who love and live with someone who has a drinking problem are living in hope. We live a life of apparent acceptance and courage, but when no one is watching we cry out our desperate fears and attempt to renew our hope.

The line between the alcoholic and the problem drinker is so fine and vague that a person can spend a lifetime trying to decide where they belong. All the time continuing to drink.

What is this madness? This compulsion that drives men and women to prove they can drink, long after they have suffered shattering effects in their own lives and the lives of those around them?

We love them. We are deeply concerned for them and their problem with alcohol. But we can't condone their anti-social or criminal behavior—or go down with them.

We love them, but we can't reach them. We can't help them until they want help. If we force help on them they will eventually return to their drinking. Out of our frustration and desperation we pray that God may in some way reach them.

Our children are growing up and leaving home to make their own way in the world—never really having known the fruits of a solid family unit. Pray God, they see the beauty of a reality and the possibility in their own lives that are beyond the misery of abuse.

They—the problem drinkers—have suffered humiliations, the inconveniences that go with drunk driving arrests, convictions and limited use of licenses. They have had to depend on others for transportation, yet they continue to drink. And they are back on the road. We fear for all those who may be on the road and in the way of someone who lacks full use of vision and wits.

This is madness!

God help us to do something about this madness before it's too late. Let's find a way to get them off the road before they kill someone.

And us, the helpless ones, who pray and wait—we know there will be help for us if we just reach out.

*   *   *

A group of adults was discussing the discipline of children when one contributor said, "When your child is rebelling against authority it is just his way of asking for discipline." I immediately volunteered, "That's what I always tell my kids before dishing out a punishment, 'You asked for it!'"

Pie on floor not in sky

I grew up with great respect for the culinary arts and its artists.

My father was a baker and to this day I believe the most pleasing aroma to be the first ovenly smell of fresh baked bread when it's taken from its final browning. Whenever I walked through the bakery where my father worked I drank in the delicious vapors and devoured numerous slices of warm bread with melting butter. They would offer me cake and cookies, but I preferred bread.

During the depression there was bread on our table when others were on welfare. My father worked long hours because people must eat, and bread was important. We never wasted a slice. Today, when bread turns green and I have to throw it away I still feel guilty. Sometimes the birds don't mind the mold.

As a child, one of my favorite bedtime snacks was torn chunks of white bread in a bowl with warm milk and sugar. No quick boxed cereal then.

I loved bread, but consider the pie to be a great work of culinary art. My mother and father used to talk about the pie shop they had in the State of Main during the depression. Times were tough and they had to give it up. They were young and they had their dreams.

I took pride in my first artistic accomplishment, a fresh peach pie. A greater challenge came many years later when I mastered the apple pie. I didn't like apple pie until I made my first one at age 19. Then I knew I was a true artist—and only I could make a really meaningful apple pie, without bits of core.

My mother insisted that all men like apple pie. When I polled friends the apple pie was in the majority. So, when I asked my husband-to-be his favorite pie I knew I would have to learn to bake the pie. I met with success and was cured.

I was in a particularly artistic mood one day. I spent two-and-a-half hours making two apple pies and a couple of shells for freezing. I tenderly placed the pies in the oven in time to dash out and pick up my kindergartner.

When the time was up I looked into the oven and beheld my two wonderful pies. One a little dark but fine. With pot-holders clutched in my hands I reached in and safely placed the largest and darkest pie on top of the stove. Then I reached in and the pot-holder didn't quite cover my wrist—so, smash went the other pie.

I'm proud of myself. I didn't even cry. Our dog, Marty, quickly came to my aid and started lapping up the applesauce off the floor. Somehow I took comfort in that gesture. I picked up some of the crust from the heap and joined Marty in sampling my realistic work of art that had suddenly become abstract art.

Men might think this whole matter insignificant. If that's the case they don't understand what the women's liberation movement is all about. It's about freedom from that kind of frustration.

On the brighter side—it's good that I made two pies.

When I viewed my smashed pie my mother's words came to mind. "Don't cry over spilled milk." I spilled a lot of milk as a kid. And, I might add, "Don't cry over smashed apple pie."

Children competing with other kids' parents

Three of my girls are working on science projects for school, and I think they've come up with some interesting subjects for their logs.

One is timing herself as she runs across the street at different times each day for a week. First in bare feet and then with her shoes on. She scratched the one with stocking feet when I protested.

Another is polling her friends and family as to their favorite color and least favorite color, and why. It makes one stop and think about how choices are made.

The third is checking the poodle out each day to see if she comes to her food or water dish first. I'm sure the dog is grateful because she can depend on eating at least once a day without being forgotten.

From the time our kids were little we refused to give them too much adult help with their projects. They have always been proud of the results because it is their own effort. But it has bothered me through the years to see projects so well finished that you know the other kids' moms or dads have given a big helping hand.

It's hard for little kids to compete with the adult skills. I certainly hope that moms and dads of Cub Scouts, Brownies, Bluebirds and other groups will let the kids do it themselves, with parental guidance.

I hope teachers and den mothers don't object, but it seems that projects should be planned according to what the child at each age can reasonably accomplish on his own. Thus eliminating the need for parents to take over.

I remember specifically the time our oldest boy was a Cub Scout and his project was to turn up with a replica of a space rocket. We figured he did a beautiful job of carving and painting his rocket. But when the rockets were displayed side by side you could tell where the dads had the skill saws and outdid the other kids.

Now read the instructions

"When all else fails, read the instructions!" I don't know where the saying originated but I know for whom it was intended. People like me.

A great deal of time and creative energy goes into the copy preparation that accompanies the manufacturer's new product to the store and into the business or home.

I love to read. I read everything that comes into the house. Even the advertising. But for some unknown reason I've developed an aversion to reading the instructions that come with a new item from the store. This is especially true in the case of small electrical appliances or the to-be-assembled small variety items.

There must be a little voice inside the box that says, "You're a know-it-all. You don't have to read the instructions. With your intelligence it's an insult."

I pretend not to listen. Eventually, when I've tried everything else on my own, I read the instructions. Down deep I know the manufacturer wants me to get the best and the most out of the product. They're not trying hard enough to convey that message as clearly as possible to even the uneducated mind. Why, oh why, do I find the instructions so hard to follow?

Adaptability of men and women to different situations

It has been said that man has superior physical stamina, greater intellectual capacity, and a relief from emotional domination. It would seem, then, that man would be more adaptable to different situations than the supposedly weak woman who is ruled by her emotions—but not so.

According to some experts woman is more adaptable to climate change, and to severe climates in many cases. She does considerably more physical exercise in her lifetime than the average American male. She is lifting, bending and stretching from dawn to dusk as a homemaking mother. She endures many physical changes due to her whole biological-chemical makeup, which most often involves the carrying, bearing and nurturing of children. She is under more physical stress during her lifetime than the average male.

Life insurance statistics find that women are living longer than men in the same age groupings. This could be a result of their physical adaptability.

Men are believed to have superior intelligence and yet complain the rest of their lives that they were "tricked" into marriage by female cunning. Their intelligence may build bridges, split atoms and fracture fractions, but they are stumped by such simple questions as, "Daddy, where do babies come from?" And they have yet to figure out what makes a woman cry, and what to do when she does.

If man is losing his place in intellectual leadership it is because he has become weaker when he should have remained strong— and woman have become stronger in areas where man wishes she had remained weak.

It is yet to be determined whether man or woman has a stronger will to overcome obstacles. The will, the most decisive factor of the human intellectual capacity is so individual that it favors neither sex, and yet both.

It has been said that woman is ruled by her emotions, yet it is man who more often indulges himself in crimes of passion, murder, rape, assault and armed robbery. Woman, by her nature, may have greater respect for human life. As a rule she is more adaptable to the marriage situation, fewer women abandon their families as compared with the greater numbers of men who disappear each year.

Women tend to accept unpleasant marital situations and adapt while the tendency on the part of the male under similar circumstances is to escape in one way or another. There is a higher rate of alcoholism and suicide among men. There are more attempts at suicide by women, but more men follow through with their threats.

Men and women are similarly equipped with a capacity for balance, for adaptability to situations but more men than women attempt to change situations rather than adapt. This is supposedly in keeping with the more active, forceful, aggressive nature of man, and the more passive, tender, home and growth centered nature of women.

There are increasing incidents of crossing over these traditional lines, where males and females each share some of the other's characteristics without losing their maleness or femaleness. Many have to learn to adapt to situations contrary to their very nature. Some have no choice in the matter, others are there by default and reluctance to change themselves or the situation.

There are no hard, fast rules at the individual level, and only a summation of conjectures on a general plane. That's the beauty of it all, men and women can be what they are meant to be, by someone else's definition. They can be what they want to be, or what they are.

The endurance test

"These are the times that try men's souls."

The refrain from our high school typing class returns again and again like a plea for help. It no longer seems necessary to quote statistics regarding the rising divorce rate, rising crime rate, rising cost of living and rising tension.

We need only look about our own neighborhoods and at our own families to see destruction nibbling away. Family foundations crumble and we remark, "I never would have believed it could happen to them." But, unfortunately, it did. And the computers gobble up another statistic.

The experts are adept at analysis in such matters. Those of us who learn by trial and error method look on with a compassionate eye and try to learn from the mistakes of others. "Into what trap did they fall? Ha! We shall avoid it." But, in practice it isn't quite so simple. It is far easier to see the wart on the end of the other guy's nose than it is to see the one starting on the end of our own nose.

Let's face it. Most marriages are a real test of endurance—for both partners. Neither husbands nor wives need break their arms patting themselves on the back for good behavior. What appears to be a failure in a relationship throws everything into a state of imbalance. "He's guilty! No, she's to blame!" And no one ever really has all the facts.

If some marriages are made in heaven, then indeed it would not be presumptuous to say that many marriages are living in hell.

Why?

Who knows for sure.

Lack of tolerance. Too many options. A desire for independence. Trying to stay together for the sake of the children and making them miserable, too.

Divorce threatens.

Is it breaking up a marriage or a family?

IV

VACATIONS, HOLIDAYS
AND OTHER HAPPENINGS

Most of us haven't grasped the meaning of leisure time. It's often more work than pleasure. Waiting for vacation time slots to relax and recreate may prove to be a deadly failing. Mothers seldom receive vacations without work and with pay, so they must learn to retreat to the pleasant resort areas of their minds. The secret places where they remind themselves of their universal worth. In the retreat of our minds we remember the events of our swift lives and savor experiences. Every day is special. Some days may be more special than others, and each day may be our last. It's worth making today our best day. Each day is a holiday of some sort, somewhere, if our vision be broad enough to perceive it as so.

Sentimental journeys

You go back a hundred times in your mind before you ever do it in person. Back to the childhood home. You don't know why, but there's something pulling and tugging and guiding your actions and footsteps when you trod the path of youth as an adult.

We never truly let go of the child inside us—after our sentimental journey we never can.

I'd been away from Michigan for 15 years, when I made my sentimental journey. I had gone back to visit my parents several times before that—once to a wedding and once to help my folks move into another house—away from the house where I'd lived nearly three quarters of my life up to that time. We made a trip back for my father-in-law's funeral, and one trip with the whole family, just for fun.

But, when I took my sentimental journey I was searching for bits of my past. My parents were settled in their new house for several years and I thought I had said good-bye to my childhood home long ago. There was a distance of nearly a mile between my parents' new house in Royal Oak, and the old house in Ferndale. Late one evening I started walking. Wasn't sure where I was going.

I arrived at the corner where I had so often boarded and stepped off the bus going to and from work. I automatically headed in the direction of "home." Walking the streets of Detroit's suburbs has never been considered safe and I reverted back to caution. Walking briskly, listening carefully, breathing heavily and looking in all directions.

While I walked, memories overwhelmed me and I became wrapped up in the emotions of the past, as an observer and as a participant.

How many others have stood outside the house they called "home" for most of their youth and wept with the sense of something lost? I had driven by the house before, but walking slowed everything down and there was time for the instant replays.

Did I find the "little girl lost?" In part.

I stood across the street looking long and hard at the house—remembering, hearing, seeing, feeling the past as though it was present. When it seemed I'd been there too long my feet followed the familiar route I'd taken to school for 11 years. A mile and a half—up the block, along the street bordering the complex of buildings that made up the chemical plant (the monster of my youth), across the railroad tracks and past numerous residences. I walked past the city library where I'd ducked in for warmth on winter days and filled up with the love of reading, past the old fire/police station and waited for the light to change at the busy intersection. Then I walked on the sidewalk along Woodward Avenue, which ran from Detroit to Pontiac, and took note of old and new buildings.

I reached the end of my journey in front of the church where I spoke my wedding vows, where the year before that I'd walked down the aisle in white cap and gown to receive a high school diploma. The church where our first child was baptized and where many of my friends and relatives received final blessings at funeral services.

I finished the journey that needed taking. For a long time to come I'll be grateful it happened. Grateful to have been in touch once more with the "girl of my past."

Vacation no break for mother of eight

Slippery when wet. Watch for falling rocks. Deer crossing. Historical marker. Elevation 3,500 feet. Gas, food, lodging next exit. Signs of travel. The most tragic sign of all reads, "Next rest area 65 miles" when a weak bladder begs expression.

If there's a particular time when I'm a real bear it's when we're trying to pack for a vacation. It doesn't matter how long the vacation will be it's still a rough time for all.

No matter how well I check the suitcases someone forgets a bathing suit, pajama top, underwear or socks. I'm usually up until the wee hours pulling it all together and I can only begin to relax once I get in the car and on the road.

It was to be our first semi-camping experience. Two nights on the concrete floor of a teepee at the Kah-nee-ta resort on the Warm Springs Indian Reservation.

Here's some advice that I will gladly pass along. One: be sure to bring an air mattress to go under the sleeping bag. I should have had a wider air mattress because I kept rolling off the sides the first night. The second night I didn't have to worry about falling out of bed, I just tried to get to sleep before all the air leaked out of the mattress.

Point two: Don't let your kids take your air mattress in the pool because they are bound to puncture yours and not theirs, and you'll end up on the concrete 10 minutes after everyone else is asleep.

You have two choices regarding temperature control inside the teepee at night. You can keep a wood fire going in the open pit stove in the center of the sleeping bag circle and wake up a dozen times to add more wood, or watch where the sparks are flying and worry about the teepee catching fire. The other choice is to crawl deep inside the sleeping bag and hope you don't suffocate.

I learned how to change my clothes inside a sleeping bag. Friendly advice from one of the young ones.

During the day there was a steady flow of traffic through the front flap of the teepee with everyone looking for grub. I know why it's called grub. It's like an underground movement getting a meal ready. No can opener, keeping the ashes from the fire out of the food, and off the floor. You have to stoop or kneel to stir vittles over an open fire or else you get smoke in your eyes and tears in the chicken noodle soup. Approach the stove with reverent caution, knowing which way the wind blows.

Clue: Put lids on all cooking pots and pans or you'll have ashes on your pancakes. I attempted to make pancakes because my campfire girl told me it would be simple. For her, maybe. I added too much water to the flour and made thin pancakes. Some of the kids were starved enough to eat them anyway. I can see why pioneer women were so proud of their cooking—edible food boasts the miraculous.

There are many ways to do the dishes. The best is to throw them away when you're finished eating. I'll bet the kids would like a dollar for every trip to the water faucet to fetch a pot full of water for dishes. We didn't have a container big enough to immerse anything but tableware, except for the ice chest. When it was empty we used it for washing dishes. Of course I forgot the detergent.

I also forgot to bring cereal bowls and the kids were good sports about eating breakfast out of glasses. No problem except that the sugar settles at the bottom and spoons don't reach.

What do you do for entertainment at night? Play Pinochle by flashlight. The one with the good eyes keeps scores. Kids have come up with new rules and subtle ways of signaling since I last played the game, but my partner and I managed to whip the cheaters with fair play and skill.

A last word of advice: Get a teepee near the rest rooms, because at 3 a.m. when a head pops out of the sleeping bag and says, "I have to go potty!" it's a fearsome sound. If it's a real emergency you may want to pop the kid into the car and drive to the place of refuge. Or else you can run like crazy with the flashlight in hand through the dark of night. The third choice—well bushes are scarce in the desert.

Add an extra plea while saying night prayers (that's when everyone is asleep and you are watching the fire for sparks) and you say, "Please God, don't let the teepee burn down tonight. Protect the bladders of my little ones. I'm grateful today is over, give me strength for tomorrow." That's the beginning camper's prayer.

Was it fun? Sure. A new experience is always worth the effort. I'd do it again, and will—but I will be smarter.

When they're quiet I worry

It's amazing the stupid things people do and how costly it can be. Last week one of the kids flushed a small plastic bottle of shampoo down the toilet by accident. It just toppled off the shelf. The plumber paid us a visit after the water level rose.

Try as he did he had to remove the entire toilet bowl and take it into the shop to get the blasted bottle out. I tried not to laugh as I watched him carry the commode out to his truck and then bring it back again later. It's no laughing matter when the bill comes.

You expect kids to do stupid things but you don't expect a grown woman to back the car out of the garage without opening the door.

It was a contest between the garage door and me. The door didn't want to stay up. When I was certain the door was secure I jumped in the car and backed out. The door fooled me. It was too late to stop. Cost: $50 (1970s prices). The damage is never beyond the insurance deductible. If a neighbor had hit the door the insurance would have paid it all. The door is now fixed so well it doesn't want to stay down without locking it.

When Paul was a young lad sharing a bedroom with his older brother he started a fire in his bed. His brother was using a bare light bulb for a science experiment and Paul thought it would be fun to play under his covers with the light on—then went off to play and left it burning.

I smelled smoke. Went down to his room and saw the light through the covers, ready to burst into flames. Fortunately Paul's room is on the ground floor because I opened the window, pulled the plug for the light, and threw the mattress out the window. Then I turned on the hose and doused the smoldering bedding. Paul got a new mattress and bedding. I'm grateful he wasn't in his bed at the time.

Then there was the time I planned a trip to Las Vegas. Two days before, one of the kids (I promised not to mention any names) swung a croquet mallet around and let it fly through the sliding glass door to the tune of $50 (1970s prices) and my mad money.

And the time Paul put the hose through the screen door and let the water run in the living room. I was on the telephone and heard water running but thought it was outside. There are times when the phone can be the enemy. The carpet had to come up and the warped floorboards had to be nailed down. Like most families we have our ups and downs.

Go fly a kite!

Adults don't have to feel guilty or silly if they enjoy the sport of kite flying. After all, big people started the whole thing.

The Chinese claim their general, Han Sin, invented the first kite for war use in 202 B.C. The Greeks may go back to 400 or 300 B.C. with the first kite.

I helped the children get their kites off the ground and questioned, who started the sport? A trip to the encyclopedia revealed that a group of grown men played around with the first kites. They claimed it was scientific. Maybe the scientific part was accidental. Someone must have thought it a lark, doing it just for fun. To justify standing with a string pointed into the air they had to defer to science.

If you sit on the bank of a pond with a fishing pole in your hand people know you're out to catch fish. But when your line is in the sky you have to come up with a better story than trying to catch birds.

Not that I'd question the motives of great men like Wilson and Melvill of Glasgow, Scotland, back in 1749, when they attached one kite to the end of the string of the other until they couldn't attach any more. They weren't fishing for birds, they were after the temperature of the clouds with a thermometer.

Benjamin Franklin fished for electricity in the sky. To date there's no report of Simple Simon fishing for pie in the sky, but he could be.

Kites gained importance in the early 1900s. The U.S. Weather Bureau used a box kite invented by Hargrave of Australia.

Birds inspired men with ideas about kites, and kites gave men ideas about airplanes. Alexander Graham Bell lifted a U.S. Army Lieutenant 175 feet into the air with the use of a large box kite. Marconi used kites to elevate the antenna at his receiving station and sent radio signals across the Atlantic Ocean in 1901.

Kite photography gained popularity. By attaching a camera to the kite photographers snapped air to ground shots as early as 1887. William Eddy took hundreds of photographs during the Spanish-American War in this manner.

When a child wants a kite for heaven's sake grant the request. Who knows, he or she may be on the way to some brilliant discovery.

So, if big people feel like flying kites, why not. It's really a big people sport that little guys have learned to love.

Body watching is fun

The human body is beautiful. A marvelous network of regulatory systems covered with skin.

Admittedly, the body is impossible to duplicate, and necessary as a package for our nervous system's signal setup. But if you're a people watcher at the beach you'll have to admit that Mother Nature has a sense of humor.

Body watching isn't reserved for men. I can't understand why some women want to show so much skin, but that's their business. It's fortunate we can abandon our self-consciousness when we get into our swimsuits.

There aren't that many men or women who look beautiful in bathing suits. Most kids look just right.

Posture is the most obvious area of neglect. My mother was always after me to straighten my shoulders. I looked undernourished enough without curling in. You might like to try my painful home remedy for keeping shoulders straight. It works for very small people.

Are you ready for this one? Obtain a hefty wire coat hanger and slip (or squeeze) it over your shoulders with the hook out front. Now, if you managed that much I defy you to curl in. You put the hook in the front so no one will sneak up behind you and grab the dumb thing and slice you in two. Not recommended for adults.

That was my shoulder straightening method for those growing years when charm school was something you read about in *Seventeen* or *Calling All Girls Magazine*. I haven't been able to convince my slouching children of the benefits of my home remedy.

Back to the bathing beauties. I hope that the next time you are at the beach in your bikini you don't feel self-conscious when people stare at your navel. Have you ever noticed the infinite variety of "belly buttons?" I used to think that was a dirty word but the dictionary merely says it's "informal."

Most kids laugh when they talk about belly buttons but most don't mind exposing one at the beach. Some appear as though the knot was tied too tight.

I bought a bikini last season but hesitate to wear it another year. Either it stretched or I shrank (could be worse, it could shrink and I could stretch). In either case I don't trust it to stay with me for may more laps.

One of the most embarrassing moments in my life was an afternoon swim in the pool at the Stardust Hotel in Las Vegas. When I took my dive off the high board my swimsuit straps snapped and I nearly drowned trying to pull it back up, fighting water power all the way. That was the beginning of the topless shows in Las Vegas, but I wasn't quite ready for it. I've stayed off the high boards ever since.

I think that people have interesting feet. There's nothing glamorous about feet—just interesting. I glanced through Sears catalogue swim section one day taking note of feet. It's seldom a striking feature on a beautiful woman, but as long as they get you where you want to go what more can you ask.

As a child I couldn't draw feet on my people. They always came out awkward and seemed to spoil the picture. Everyone had Minnie Mouse type shoes or long skirts. I avoided feet with a passion. I covered them with sand or a blanket.

Next time you take your body to the beach remember that skin is shallow and beauty is in the soul of the owner.

Cures for the "nothing to do" syndrome

Summertime and life gets boring for youngsters. Mother is getting housemaid's knees scrubbing the kitchen floor when the little darlings burst into their refrain, "There's nothing to do."

The last thing in the world they want to fill their empty moments with is the nasty four-letter word, w-o-r-k.

I learned that lesson early in life. Don't go to your mother when there's nothing to do because she'll find something for you to do that you don't want to do. Boredom pushed me back on my own initiative and resourcefulness.

Friends couldn't play, gone for the day, or playing with someone else and no room for one more. The "nothing to do" syndrome was more of an appeal to recognition and acceptance.

How to fill lonely, empty hours?

Number one has always been reading. Second, jump on a bike and ride as far as I could before getting tired. Climb off the bike and sit down in a quiet field somewhere and dream or cry. After exhausting the "poor me" syndrome you can relax and enjoy listening to the grass grow or watch the clouds move about making puffy images in the sky. You can always find a Snoopy. Then make up stories to go with the pictures you see out there in space.

If you're not old enough to take the adventuresome bike ride you might try a trip around the block on a three-wheeler, or a slow walk to see what you missed the last time around.

Children don't seem to play with paper dolls or cut-outs anymore. We used to design clothes for homemade paper dolls, then make up dramatic scenes to put them into action.

Too often when children come to us and say "there's nothing to do" we direct them to the television instead of challenging their imaginations with the kind of things that used to keep us busy and happy.

I don't favor the voo doo doll concept, but you can take out a lot of frustration with a couple of stuffed animals.

We made pot holders in the summer recreation program. Learned to use a saw, hammer, nails and paint. There were woodburning sets, paints, paper and pencil, crayons and coloring books, and a deck of playing cards. Would you believe I've only won a few game of Solitaire in my life, but I keep trying.

Get out all the old magazines and cut out pictures to make a scrap book or a collage. Sit on the floor and play jacks. What happened to all the games that could be played with a bouncy rubber ball? Why don't girls and boys jump rope anymore? It's almost guaranteed that when you draw a hop-scotch on the pavement and look as though you're having a great time a playmate will emerge from hiding and want to play.

If all else fails make faces at yourself in the bathroom mirror, with the door locked. Sit in a quiet corner and daydream. Why are big and little folks so afraid of being caught thinking and dreaming? Try on old clothes belonging to Mother or Dad. Dress up the dog. Take the dog for a walk. Stare at the fish in the aquarium and try to figure out which are males and females. Clean out a closet or drawer and be amazed at finding lost treasures. Think of it as a treasure hunt, not work. Take your little brother or sister for a walk.

Sew on a button. Search for four leaf clovers in the lawn. Climb a giant tree and make like an owl. String beads, collect bottle caps, make a ball of string, watch the aphids eat the roses, look for frogs in the weeds, play school, read last Sunday's comics again, start a rock collection, run up the street without stepping on a sidewalk crack.

Whatever you do, if you're smart, don't ask your mother for something to do because chances are it will be work and not play she has in mind.

Litterbugs mar remote forest areas

Trees so tall that I grew dizzy trying to see the tops. Water rushed off the rocks and ran down the side of the road, water icy to the touch. Roads into the wilderness area went from rough to worse.

In January, when I promised to drive my oldest son and his friends to their backpacking site in the Mt. Hood National Forest, I had no idea what I was getting myself in for.

We left the house at 7:30 a.m. and I returned, hot and haggard, at 3:30 p.m. Allowing time out for eating, getting gas for the car, getting off on the wrong roads and letting the car cool, it was still pretty good time. I was to pick them up a week later at the same trailhead.

Panic is getting lost in the forest. Your sense of security suddenly vanishes when the whole dashboard lights up red after going five miles an hour on a jagged rock road for two miles.

We were still two thirds of a mile from the spot where they wanted to start their hike and I couldn't convince them to walk that extra bit and give the car a break. I stopped the car when the steering wheel and brakes locked. I opened the hood of the car and listened to the bubbling and gurgling of hot motor parts. And I prayed. It was 20 miles to the nearest gas station.

Don't panic! I told myself. Just cool it.

The car cooled and the red lights went out. I drove the boys the rest of the way in and circled back for my trip downhill. Two miles on jagged rock and about 10 miles of gravel later I reached the dirt road that led to civilization. When I touched down on black top it was a great feeling.

I love the clean mountain air, the green trees and cold streams and lakes—but I'd like them to be a bit closer to a gas station. My son tells me the remoteness is what preserves the area. On the way up the hill the boys discussed the benefits of bad roads, claiming it kept people away and kept the wilderness untouched. I suppose even the wilderness areas can become crowded with so many people heading there to be alone with nature.

The backpacking experience must be worthwhile because my son was returning to the same trail he hiked the year before. At that time he took pictures and I was impressed and envious. If there was an easier way to get back to Twin Lakes, Welcome Lake and Bull of the Woods, I would go.

The inaccessibility of these lakes preserves them from pollution.

On the way down hill, on the dusty road, I stopped at the point where the boys filled their canteens on the way up. Water rushed over the rocks like small waterfalls. I kicked off my shoes, sat on a rock, and dangled my feet in the water until my toes turned to icicles. I ate the sandwich my son shared with me from his pack. It was nearly 100 degrees in the sun and I appreciated the pleasant quiet of the time and place.

I headed back to the car and looked over the other side of the road where water poured through a huge drainpipe, and there was an empty carton from a case of beer.

Mother reads *Playboy Magazine*

Whenever I travel I buy a newspaper to get the local color. It's not necessarily a true mirror of the personality of the community, but it comes close to providing insights through news format and editorial content.

On a recent trip down the coast by auto we stopped for an early morning breakfast in the middle of nowhere. I picked up a San Francisco paper and an advertisement for *Playboy Magazine* caught my eye. They boasted about an interview with Governor Jerry Brown (1970s) and I was extremely curious about the man's political philosophy and the state's administrative practices. In addition, I'm always interested to see how other interviewers handle their subject. I'd read reprints of previous *Playboy* interviews and respected the quality of the prose.

It pained me to put the money on the counter of a little grocery/liquor store down the street from Disneyland two days later. I detest the sexual exploitation on the pages of the magazine and am uncomfortable with the big bosom fixation. I think it's sexist.

So, I was on vacation and feeling daring. I put the *Playboy Magazine* on top of the Sunday paper that was wrapped in multicolored comics. I thumbed through the magazine to make sure it contained the Governor Brown article. The clerk asked, "What's *Playboy* writing about Brown for, he some kind of a pervert?"

"No, he's clean," I reacted like a voice of authority. I resented being questioned about my purchase. I grabbed the newspaper and magazine and made my exit as the clerk and another man laughed behind my back.

I tore the article out of the magazine and read it by the pool the next day. "Hey everybody, my mom reads *Playboy*," a voice shouted out of the pool and I cringed.

School—glad to have you back

Summer's nearly over and we're grateful for many things.

Once again we begin to organize our lives around a schedule, and for me that's a blessing. I need time slots and pegs on which to hang my plans during the day, instead of the revolving door routine and breakfast every hour until noon.

It's wonderful to have 12 weeks of summer to be at loose ends, if you can stand it. The glow wears off about mid-August when restlessness sets in. Children start planning for school clothes, supplies and getting in touch with school friends.

From mid-August on is busy time for moms. It's a major task trying to get kids outfitted for school and still have enough money left for Christmas time when it rolls around.

Kids have been going barefoot all summer and their feet have grown. The price of shoes goes up every year and kids refuse to wear cardboard from Shredded Wheat boxes inside to cover the hole in the sole. Fact is they usually grow out of them before they wear the shoes out. Kids don't even want to wear mended socks anymore. They think poverty means you don't have a built-in swimming pool or a theater-size TV screen.

Freezing and canning certain fruits and vegetables coincides with return to school. Dollar-wise it may be worth canning, but it becomes an increasingly costly and lost art. There may be more pride in six jars of pickles you did yourself than in a case bought on sale at the grocery store. There is also pride in seams of a dress made by hand and sewing machine.

Many of our young people are moving back to the land. Back to unenriched, unfortified and unsaturated living. In this world of mechanical great things I want the best of both the old and the new—the flavor and savor of the past and the convenience of the present. At times I envy the less complicated way of living enjoyed by many.

With the approach of school, structure returns. There will be at least one meeting a week, and the pressing schedule of my own activities. Back to busy lives.

I'm not necessarily in favor of year-around school but we do need more options available to us. We can't possibly entertain children for a whole summer. Some of them can find jobs, but far too many can't. There are recreation and study programs available during the first part of summer but everything dies down in August. We can't all go on vacation in August.

Away with the faded and worn bathing suits. Up with the memories of sand and surf and good times. Gone are the days of dripping wet towels and suits from one end of the house to the other. Watery footsteps in the hall have nearly disappeared. Water fights in the backyard give way to other sports and to homework assignments.

Ah, summer, I love you. But then again the autumn has its beautiful moments, and change of pace.

Daily battles bring retreat

I've just returned from a private retreat. When a person grows weary of doing daily battle and feels the need to fall back from enemy lines for a time, regroup and fortify, then they retreat. At times it's best to go it alone.

I retreated from the world of television sets, radios, newspapers, children, and all the other things and people that I spend most of my time with or around. I went away from Friday night until Sunday afternoon to gain relaxation and spiritual fortification.

I occupied a guest room at a monastery. No one to sermonize to me. No schedules except to eat. I wasn't sure I could handle the quiet and non-structure.

I slept a great deal, and a person should be grateful for the healing effects of a good sleep. It gives the mind a chance to slow down and reorganize.

When you're faced with a quiet room where the ticking of the clock is your companion, what do you do?

First of all you come face to face with yourself. Then you make some effort at communication with God. And suddenly you remember that He has been there all along but you were just too busy to notice, or the TV was too loud for Him to get through. So, there you are and you wonder who is supposed to make the first move. You begin to realize that He's already made many first moves that you've been too busy to appreciate.

Then you struggle. Finding a channel of communication. Praying. Listening. A two-way job.

Maybe when people complain that they can't pray they're just poor listeners. Think of all the noise and confusion we have to overcome to be heard—or to hear.

We have to listen for God's voice with the ears of our heart, and that takes effort. Maybe we're all afraid of the silence, afraid to be alone with God, afraid of what He may say to us.

I took long walks, spent a reasonable amount of time in the chapel, ate hearty meals, read some, wrote some, and slept my fair share. Doesn't sound very exciting, does it? That's what's so great.

It's like stopping the world and getting off for a couple of days, getting your bearings and climbing back on again.

Excuse me while I let my halo out a notch—I think my head grew.

Getting rid of some of the cobwebs left space to move around in that little room inside my head.

Twenty-year reunion for class of 1951

There may be a tendency on the part of many to discount high school class reunions as so much illusion and disappointment.

Illusion exists for some alumni who may tip too many cocktail glasses or fail to see beyond the excitement of the moment. As for disappointment, that has to be very individual; perhaps not what one finds at the party but what they brought with them.

There was nothing disappointing about the 20-year class reunion that I will cherish the rest of my days. If my expectations for the event were high then they were met or exceeded. Illusion is inescapable because time doesn't allow in-depth interviews with each person attending, but I covered as much as possible in a brief period of time.

People are wonderful and interesting. Whatever else must be said about reunions we have to admit they satisfy our innate curiosity about how time has treated those we knew long ago.

Information and gossip flooded the room. Some of the old cliques were still gathering together, but on the whole perspectives had broadened considerably with maturing. It was a time to catch up on who is married to whom, how many children, occupations, joys and sorrows. Who lost their healthy head of hair and who gained weight? White hair, illnesses, and even deaths were news. From a class of 69 students more than 50 percent made the reunion.

The St. James High School closed its doors the year before our reunion. It bit the dust raised by financial crisis in private education. Signs of troubled times.

Many of my classmates went on to success. Our class president invested his time in law enforcement, climbing the Michigan State

Police ladder. One of his remarks to me carried the significance of the times in which we were living. Two of his troopers went to the hospital the day before with injuries received in the line of duty.

"Marilyn, I have had many men die in my arms. This kind of life has taught me two things, to be humble and grateful."

Another classmate invested 15 years in police work in Detroit. When the burning, rioting and looting broke out the end of the 1960s, and lives, homes and families of policemen were on the line he decided someone else would have to save the world. He moved to a farm and keeps nine milking cows working.

Another classmate made a career of state police work, and another became an attorney, and then a judge. There were several in the field of education, including three nuns. I hope in the years to come that my book-buyer friend will include my work on her list.

I won an ice bucket for traveling the farthest. My best friend, maid of honor at my wedding, and godmother to my oldest child also received an ice bucket for coming the second farthest from Kansas. Three tied for the most children, with nine. I wasn't even in the running with my eight.

There were lots of laughs, lost sleep and sharing of memories. When the nostalgia sets in I'll play the audio tape of the off-the-cuff dinner remarks. I made a copy of the tape for my girlfriend in California who couldn't make the trip.

I traveled to Michigan with an empty cup of curiosity and returned with an overflow of memories.

Now, more 30 years later, I'm even more grateful, since I missed my 50-year reunion. We were in the Portland airport at 6 a.m. on September 11, 2001. The plane never took off for Detroit. My friend from California got as far as Las Vegas, and two days later was able to continue her trip. It was a very sad and tragic time for our country and for each of us, individually.

Escapism of sports and realism of injuries

I was hard pressed to keep up with the weekend sports pace.

I'm worn to a frazzle from watching the Portland Trailblazers basketball team going down to defeat in their opening game. Cheering Oregon State University on to victory against Arizona on the football field, and listening to the radio broadcast of the Oregon and Washington gridiron game. Getting reports from the Buckaroo hockey game, and catching some TV coverage of the Major League Baseball World Series.

A great escape time. Baseball winds up, hockey and basketball begin, and football goes on and on, and on.

There's something for everyone in our sports loving nation. Fortunately those who can't afford tickets can still enjoy events on radio and television.

I was raised on Detroit Tiger baseball and made difficult adjustments in California without a major league team for several years. Then the Dodgers came to Los Angeles and we had to learn how not to call them "Bums." Now, in the Oregon outpost, we toss a coin to choose a favorite team at World Series time.

Americans must spend a striking amount of money on sports entertainment. For some reason baseball always struck me as the poor man's sport. As a kid we occasionally lined up for the cheap bleacher seats, but most often Dad got tickets off the first or third base lines. When I was a kid I thought people who went to college or to pro-football games were rich. I was a senior in high school before I saw my first college football game; University of Detroit hosted Notre Dame for an exhibition game in the coliseum.

Everyone plays baseball. Football has had more glamour attached to it. Each sport appeals to a segment of the population and has its good points. A new kind of "football" has come upon the scene in America. In the Portland area the public has taken soccer to its heart. In the first year of play the attendance increased and multiplied and amazed everyone—especially the initial investors who banked on public acceptance of the new Portland Timbers Soccer Team.

We had watched our eldest son play soccer for four years in high school and we were ready to go when the Timbers arrived. It was a family summer of soccer and we cheered them on to capture division and regional titles. Two of our girls played soccer in high school. They sacrificed glamorous looking legs for bruises and shin splints during the fast paced season. And, it's the game that excites them, both watching and playing.

People get hurt in soccer but I haven't seen the kinds of injuries viewed in American football. I always found it disturbing to see a player carried off the football field. I guess when your whole purpose is to stop the other guy by crashing right into him then someone is bound to get hurt occasionally. Injuries in basketball and baseball are usually minor by comparison.

If there's a sport I really hate it's the manly art of self-defense—boxing. I've never been able to get into the excitement of two grown men beating each other's brains out. There's a lot of money in boxing and it has its appeal to the poor kid who fights his way up to the top. Boxing isn't that far removed from the Roman gladiators' combat.

Two sports I avoid with a passion are the Saturday Night Roller Derby and the wrestling matches. The theatrics of the two have given sportsmanlike wrestling and good roller skating bad names. There's little femininity in women's roller derby to be sure. Over 20 years ago (now 40 years ago) when television first came out the wrestling and roller derby were popular, mainly because most of the programming was poor. We've made advances since then, but some folks still cling to the old forms of entertainment. I guess that's their privilege.

With all the money spent on sports there must, indeed, be a great therapeutic effect upon us all. It must supply some outlet for our emotions, some escape from day-to-day challenges.

Those are real people on the fields, courts, diamonds and ice—and in the ring as well. They do a real job of performing and entertaining the public. And I, for one, know it has been good therapy on many occasions to scream at an umpire rather than at my kids. Maybe it's a better way of relieving tension than some other ways we might choose.

Mementos from Mother's Day

M is for my mother.
O is for often taking us places.
T is for touching, it shows you care.
H is for the hope you have.
E is for everlasting love.
R is for remembering us.

One of my beautiful daughters brought her message home from school and it is treasured along with a similar message from her sister.

M is for the marvelous things you do.
O is for the only mother I want.
T is for the terrific way you cook.
H is for the hard work you do.
E is for energetic.
R is for the running around you do.

Although their attitude toward me may change many times through the year, and the years, at least I will know they once felt some warmth and appreciation.

"Be good to your mother. She's the only one you have, and when she's gone she's gone!" I heard my own mother say this to me many times during my growing years. For the most part she used her own mother as an example.

No matter how we feel about the real or imagined harm we believe our mothers inflicted upon us, we owe them a great deal for giving us life. For a fact, we owe our fathers a thank you, too. But I think we all recognize that a woman's part in bringing life into the world is far more complex and involving than that of the man.

Mothers aren't perfect. Giving birth doesn't insure that a woman will do all the right things in raising her children. But, we are very much alive and we have a mother to thank for that.

The "wanted" and the "unwanted" child has been the subject of much debate, and sometimes traumatic for the one who determines he or she is in the latter grouping. Children are a tremendous inconvenience in our lives but that doesn't seem a good enough reason to deny them an existence. Perhaps I did have to alter some of my plans to allow for pregnancy—eight times—but the children are all loved and accepted. Even those who protest that they must be adopted because of what they consider poor treatment by their parents.

Children often argue and fight and a mother finds it distressing. Perhaps friction rubs the corners smooth. I tell them that when they get older they'll really appreciate each other. I hope.

For the first 10 years of my life I had a brother who was 15 months older than me. We were close. My parents and my brother and I did many things together. We were a strong unit. Then my brother drowned as we were swimming one Sunday afternoon in June of 1943. (Subject of previous book *Little Girl Lost*.)

I knew what it was like to have a brother—and I know what it's like to grow up without that companionship. It became my wish that I would never have an only (or lonely) child. Some would say I overdid it.

I don't consider myself a special mother—but I do feel that motherhood is very special. We're not divided down the middle and playing mother role now, career role later, and wife role. They all roll into one person and fit together—sometimes with some major and minor adjustments and squeezing.

Mothers! For all their faults, where would we be without them?

Happy Birthday U.S.A.!

Those of us who were born in the United States of American salute you, and those who have come to your shores from all over the world to adopt you as their own land salute you.

You're not perfect, but we love you. To the suffering, oppressed, hungry and poor in the rest of the world you are still a vision of refuge, a vision of freedom.

You are still youthful as a government and a country. Yet you walk tall with a long list of accomplishments that most of the world envies.

Many immigrated to your shores. They sought a better way of life. You embraced them, your adopted children. We, your children by birth, welcome them into our family—remembering that those who came before us came from other lands. Many have unique stories to tell.

Mrs. Van Der Zanden embraced citizenship. She was born in Czechoslovakia of German parents. She was 16 when they were forced to leave their country because of occupation by Russian soldiers in 1946. She was separated from her family for nine months. During that time she was employed in Austria. Later she joined her family in Germany, only to leave that all behind in 1956 when she came to the United States.

"For some reason I knew there must be a better place to live." Mrs. Van Der Zanden had contacts in the U.S.A., aunts who had encouraged her to come. She promised herself she'd become a U.S. citizen "five years and one day" after entering. She became a citizen, proud of the work she did to pass the test. Then she went back to Germany to visit her family, as an American citizen.

"When I opened my passport for the first time and saw that I was the property of the United States—I can't describe the feeling. It is too bad people don't really appreciate what we have here. I guess you have to live somewhere else first—to know another way of life—before you do."

In 1949 there were 14 Catholic nuns living in China. Communism was making advances. They fled, leaving family, friends and possessions behind. Six months later the Communists took over their convent and property.

Twenty years later, six of those nuns became American citizens after 10 weeks of preparation in night classes. When asked about the value of citizenship one of the nuns replied, "We don't want to live under communism. In China there is no freedom. The people have no priests, no sacraments, nothing to eat." Her own father was killed by the Communists in 1947 and her brother, a Jesuit priest, was in a Communist prison in China for more than 15 years.

Another nun said, "We want freedom to do what we wish, what is right." She hopes that China will someday have peace "as we have it."

Another nun is grateful to George Washington "who established our country—a free country—where we come to serve people for the honor and glory of God. In China . . . no religious freedom."

Nicholas and the spirit of Christmas

Nicholas was a compassionate young man. Comparatively speaking he was wealthy, at least quite comfortable for the fourth century after the birth of Christ.

Nicholas lived in a small community in Asia Minor. He couldn't hide his concern for the welfare of his needy neighbors. But he did try to hide the help he offered them. At night he went out and placed food, clothing or money at the houses of those he knew were poor.

On one particular occasion he overheard a poor father's lament that his daughters and he were near starvation. The daughters pleaded with their father to let them go into the streets and beg. The father was a man of faith and told them to wait one more day, and he prayed that God would save his children from the disgrace of begging.

Nicholas dug into his inheritance and on three successive nights secretly provided the family with funds. On the third night Nicholas was caught. The father fell at his feet, cried, and thanked him for his kindness.

Nicholas told the man to thank God, because that was who sent him to their aid. This young man had a great desire to do good for others and a corresponding desire to remain hidden while doing good. The young man later became a priest. He wished to live in the Holy Land, but on a return trip from there he was informed he was elected the Bishop of Myra.

As bishop Nicholas continued to be the essence of compassion and giving. He became the protector of the innocent and the oppressed.

The loving and giving spirit of Nicholas was contagious. But

Nicholas was quick to admit that he was only sharing what he had been given. He said his own loving spirit was the result of someone else giving him an overflow. Nicholas was the living spirit of Christmas for his time and place.

Because God has compassion He gave us Christmas. And Nicholas gave Christmas to his people. After his death many people believed that good things happened to them because they begged the very memory, or spirit, of Nicholas for help.

Nicholas was a very influential man while he was with his people, but after his death that influence spread to other parts of the world.

Nicholas of Myra has been known as a patron saint of Greece, and with St. Andrew, is a patron of Russia. There are nearly 400 pre-reformation English churches dedicated in his name.

We still honor the spirit of Christmas by honoring St. Nicholas. Many people believe as the young Nicholas did, that they want to hide their gift giving. So, in hiding the good things they do for others they receive a double joy.

Capture whatever fragments of that true Christmas spirit that you can. Hold it close and let it warm your heart because this one moment may never happen again.

Hold on to enough of that spirit of warmth in giving, and in leaving yourself open for receiving, to last through the coming year. There will be times when it will be most welcome.

Life's a stage for bit players

Each year parents witness the dramatic and musical efforts of their children of all ages. I've tried to convince my children that supporting roles are important and necessary, and that someone has to do it.

Tryouts for the lead in the Christmas play are completed. Selections made. Tears wept. Supporting roles and behind the scenes duties assigned. And it all comes together.

If fame ever comes to me I'll always remember that I started out as a clothes pole. My mother told me that my first dramatic effort in kindergarten was holding up one end of the line for the "four and twenty blackbirds" who eventually ended up in a pie. How's that for a supporting role?

I'm convinced I performed well as a clothes pole, and my line didn't sag.

Later I went on to fame as an angel. That was before they found out about type casting. And another year along in my career I dressed the part for an Indian doll who came to life at the magic moment with all the other dolls in the toy store. The following year I was miscast as an Irish doll. That was the year I blew my big chance to do a solo, "I've got a pain in my sawdust." My voice was too weak, so another girl went on to lose her stuffings instead of me. But, for some reason my stomach hurt when she sang.

The eighth grade was my big year. We performed in Dickens' *Christmas Carol*. I did everything from painting scenery to prompting in the wings when friends forgot their lines. I had three bit parts. One was so small that I've forgotten what it was.

My mother curled my hair in rags and I played the little girl in Scrooge's past. Then I pulled a stocking cap over my curly head of hair, and put on a pair of knickers to sell Scrooge a turkey after his conversion to a nice guy from an old grump.

I can't recall ever playing a lead part, but I do know that I always enjoyed being a part of the acting scene.

Gifts from the hand, the heart or the hearth

There are seasons of handmade gifts. Seasons when people grow tired of giving store bought goodies that break too soon or become conveniently lost.

Every year we get all wrapped up in the buying and wrapping and have saved little time or energy to give the most precious gifts of all—gifts that require something of our very selves.

Children bring us their handmade offerings from school and there is some show of appreciation for their efforts, but somehow they soon learn that greater value is placed on those items that cost great numbers of dollars. We've become accustomed to thinking in terms of bigger and bigger gifts. Pieces of furniture, cars, audio-visual-video electronic equipment, gift certificates, and electrical appliances of all kinds.

A good friend told me her family made a rule many years ago that they would only exchange gifts that were hand made, or something from the pen or brush, or baked in the oven or on the stovetop.

I remember a happy Christmas Eve when my brother received an electric train. I got a large baby doll, and we both sported new Mickey Mouse watches. It was years later before I knew how hard it was for my parents to pay for the train. Mother put the train on lay-away in the summer and paid a dollar a week until Christmas.

Dolls are okay, but I favored trains. The doll lasted until I passed it on to my own first little girl and she allowed a friend to play with it. The doll came home with a cracked head from an airplane ride, and I wept.

The train? Well, I really don't know where the train ended up. My brother died the following summer and we packed the train away. Eventually my mother gave it to another little boy. I like to think he treasured it as much as we did, my brother and I.

*   *   *

When we were kids we begged our parents to take us for a drive at night to see the Christmas lights in the rich parts of Detroit. Now there are as many lights in our neighborhood as any we saw when we were kids. I wish my kids appreciated what it means to me.

Safety in toys

Children's toys have become so complex that it takes a note of caution in selection—and even supervising the use of some. Older children may get toys or games that should be kept out of the hands of the little ones.

Dart boards and chemistry sets enter the dangerous category

in the wrong hands. Dart boards often fall apart in a matter of months, but the darts linger on. I've cleaned up a large lump of some colorful mixture poured from several bottles. The remains of the chemistry set ended up on the storage room floor when little hands gained access. Fortunately it was the floor and not the stomach that got the deposit.

Toys with small parts or marbles eventually get stepped on by one of the barefooted brood to the tune of screams and yelps. Straight pins that hold clothing neatly in place while packaged can stick nicely in the carpet just waiting for tender toes and heels. Any type of pop-gun or toy that shoots objects can be potentially dangerous if aimed near the eyes. It doesn't hurt to examine some of the metal toys for rough edges that might cut little fingers.

Toys should be entertaining and sometimes educational, not dangerous. They should also be peaceful. We talk a good deal about peace and I think there's a lot to be said for discouraging guns as toys.

A fine lady from England remarked to me that "children should not be taught that it is fun to kill." I heartily agree. She'd gone through the bombing years in London during World War II, and saw nothing "fun" about weapons.

There's another consideration about toy buying. How much noise does it make? For the sake of my own tender ears I search for quiet toys.

Toys can be fun and still be safe.

Children grow up and leave home

Our family is getting smaller.

The day comes when we must realize that our children have grown up. This usually comes on moving day. Their moving day.

Our oldest daughter is now an apartment dweller. We've been cooperatively working toward her moving day for several months—then it happened on New Year's Eve.

Suddenly the arguments about who would get her room ceased. The decision was made and two happy teen-agers got their rooms to themselves after sharing with younger brother or sister for years. Hopefully everyone will be happy with the moves.

Everyone wanted the room when it was vacated. I reached the point of threatening to rent it out and let everyone stay where they were. I made a diagram of the children's five bedrooms. Then cut out five pink squares of paper for the girls and two blue squares for the boys. Everyone had a go at shifting the papers around on the diagram to arrive at a satisfactory solution.

Children grow up. I did, and mine are. It's not traumatic unless you've been holding on too tight. In a large family everyone has responsibilities. The oldest generally has more responsibility. They also have more privileges and freedom.

It's difficult to say when you stop treating children like children and start treating them as adults. It takes many years of preparing them for independence by giving it, or letting them take it, a little at a time.

Independence is a two-way thing. Parents have to learn a loving detachment from their children. You can't make your children your whole life because those children grow up and grow away. With the mobility in our society those children may move thousands of miles away. As I did. My parents were 2,385 miles away.

There's certainly a feeling of relief when you've raised the oldest child to the threshold of adulthood. You turn the worry over to them. They are now responsible to themselves for what they do. They may stretch their philosophy of living far afield from what they've been taught at home, but it takes time to make those adjustments. Time and experience.

The time comes to put away the things of a child. We all hold tightly to childhood dreams, keepsakes, memories. We're so anxious to grow up that we begin to abandon the keepsakes one by one for new ones. We're so anxious, and just as fearful

And when our oldest daughter comes for dinner, as she did today, I will probably always ask her to "Please mash the potatoes."

V

PURSUING HEALTH, WEALTH AND HAPPINESS

There aren't any constitutional guarantees in this department. Although we all agree that health and wealth are great aids to happiness they don't bring it about. Happiness, like the immortal, mythical Phoenix Bird who rises fresh and beautiful from its own ashes, becomes increasingly evasive the more it is pursued. Often happiness happens when we lose ourselves in helping others to survive.

Staying healthy at home

More than half of all the women between 18 and 64 years of age work outside the home (1970s statistics). There are fewer stay-at-home wives and mothers all the time. Those who stay home may do it by choice and sometimes by necessity. It's their career.

Many dads are choosing to stay at home and be the homemaker. Other dads are adjusting their schedules to share in child raising and home making.

Young mothers at home caring for their children as well as full-time or part-time working mothers often neglect their own health because they're too busy meeting the needs of others. Although the homemaker isn't paid by the hour, economists estimate her monetary value in the neighborhood of $14,000 per year, were her services to be purchased. (Multiply that 1976 estimate by three decades in the rising cost of living.) Dollar figures alone are good reason to take care.

Your home can be your gym. Look around at the possibilities. Doorways to stretch arm muscles. Beds to make and exercise bending and reaching correctly. Cupboards in the kitchen to practice leg-bends. Open windows and doors to practice deep breathing. Deep breathing is the most vital and most neglected exercise of all. If you're lonesome exercising turn on the half hour Yoga or bend and stretch exerciser of your choice early in the morning, or get a video.

What you eat or don't eat can make or break you. Fatigue? A teaspoon of honey or a handful of raisins or nuts can provide more nutrition and energy than a candy bar or a piece of cake. Make substitutes for weaknesses.

Everyone needs a change of pace. Don't stick at one boring job too long. Don't sit or stand too long at a time if you can help it. Alternate working positions. Plan to empty the garbage at 10 a.m. if it will help get you out of the house for a few minutes. Take the baby or toddler for a stroll before lunch to get you both some fresh air and exercise.

Personal care is healthy fun. Every woman enjoys looking her best. So what if you want your husband or mate to know how hard you worked all day! You don't have to look like you've been down in the mine shaft to make it convincing. He can probably tell by the way you, the house and the kids look, even if he doesn't give you praise. Besides, if you look good he won't notice lunch dishes in the sink.

Relax! It won't happen unless you plan it. One woman's work is another woman's relaxation. Decide what gives you that sense of refreshment and work it into your schedule. Feet propped on the coffee table at 3 p.m., a shower at 4 p.m., a phone call to a friend you haven't seen in eons, or several grand moments of silence— even if it takes earplugs. Let the mind drift and snooze.

Emotional ups and downs can play havoc with your psychology, and with the family atmosphere. So what, we're entitled to a good cry occasionally. Let 'er rip! It's better than holding everything back and making yourself and everyone else miserable. But be done with it. Finish! Enough is enough. How long can you feel weepy and constructive?

Now that you've had a good cry. Or perhaps it's a good old-fashioned cupboard door slamming session, kicking clothes down the stairs, or beating the rug. You may discover ways of planning the frustration-letting sessions, perhaps a trip to the tennis court or swimming pool, or jump rope in the back yard. We have to work with what we have on hand and available to us.

Ouch, those hormone hills and valleys. Monthly mood changes. (Though it's a closely guarded secret men also have mood changes.) So, you've got 'em. Learn how to deal with them. Granted, it is easier said than done. Recognize symptoms of mood changes and learn how to avert, sidetrack or derail some of those horrible dips into depression.

Call a friend, scrub a floor, read a book, have lunch in the park, watch for changing shapes in the clouds while laying in the tall grass your husband forgot to cut, pick up the baby and study the fine structure of miniature fingers and beautiful eyes.

If you're given to spiritual moments of meditation, transcendence, being at one with the universe, communicating with a higher power, realizing your own human potential or inner strength—make the most of it. Work it into your day. A time for coming to grips with your place in the time-space thing and your journey onward and upward.

Put it all together. Get your body cooperating with your mind and out of it comes a human spirit that can fly with the wind and go where it wills. Generate love with your inner machinery. You'll become more important to others when you find your source of strength and learn how to give it away.

A happier, healthier you is a tremendous asset to the universe.

Preventive health measures cost less

Illness has created one of the biggest supply and demand businesses in our country, and by now everyone realizes that without adequate hospital and medical coverage the cure (or cost of) could prove more fatal than the original problem.

I was signing the final papers for my daughter's release from the hospital after her tonsillectomy when a nurse wheeled by a man with a smile on his face and holding two potted plants.

"What floor do you go to with a heart attack?"

The attending nurse answered his question and then asked why. He replied that that was where he'd probably be going after he saw his bill.

A realist to be sure. So, back to the ounces of prevention that are worth pounds of cures.

Most people abuse and waste their bodies. When they have good health they lack the appreciation and care. I was one of those teenagers who thought she could run off to school on a bowl of dry cereal, gulp down a lunch so I could spend more time socializing, get supper when and where it was convenient because of extra-curricular activities and working.

I have a fine mother who tried to tell me I was ruining my health and would regret it. Yet, I saw nothing wrong with keeping up the hectic pace that everyone else seemed to thrive on. I saw nothing wrong with a full week of school and a full weekend of working and social life. Many a time I went from school on Friday to my job at the bakery counter in the grocery store until someone came by to take me to a party or a dance, followed by an all-night pajama party. In the morning I crept out of the house while the others still slept. Then I took a bus or buses to be at work by 7 a.m. and get the bakery counter set up for the Saturday rush of customers.

And that was only the beginning of the weekend.

There is something amazingly impenetrable about the teenage mind. And I paid dearly for the joy of youth. Unfortunately we don't seem to obtain sufficient wisdom early enough in our lives to avoid this massive abuse of human resources. Sometimes, when people take proper care of their bodies they may be accused of being food-fad fanatic or a health nuts. But, times are changing, and people are becoming more realistic.

It's hardly ever too late to start repairing what we've done to our bodies. The road to regaining health is far more rugged than the road of maintaining good health.

I'm speaking primarily about the majority of people who can and should do more toward their good health. Are we a nation of do-it-to-yourselfers in every area except the ones where we can make a difference? Do too many of us wait until we've sufficiently run the body down like an old car battery or set of worn tires, and then find a physician to put us back together?

How many men keep working when they should give their bodies a rest? How many of us stay up late at night watching some old movie on TV when we should be in our beds? And there are the breakfast skippers who start a full day on an empty stomach laced with a cup of black coffee. Not much nourishment there, nor for that matter in the after work martini, unless you count the olive.

There's hardly one among us who can cast a stone when it comes to self-abuse, and the medical profession is hard pressed to keep the supply in line with the demand.

It must be discouraging for doctors to realize that their patients aren't taking their advice. But then, they can pout all the way to the bank. Who do people think they are fooling when they report to their doctor that they have followed their diets, quit smoking or drinking, and generally changed their lifestyle? In their slavery to habit they lie. Ah well, that's life—and sometimes death.

Rights of non-smokers

Air pollution control begins with the smoker. I've got a right to breathe clean air. So, put that in your pipe and smoke it.

I quit smoking the hard way, and though I sympathize with the smoker I don't want to inhale second-hand smoke. There are several good reasons why I should have quit smoking sooner.

1. I was 18. Sat in the back seat of my parents' car on the return trip from Maine to Michigan. The windows were open to allow air in on a hot day. I lit my cigarette and forgot to "close cover before striking" the match. The whole book of matches flared up in my hand. I burned my thumb

and several fingers enough to be painful as hell but not enough to require medical attention.

2. My husband-to-be didn't smoke and begged me to quit before we were married. I said okay but still smoked on occasion, but not in his presence. I hid my smokes among the diapers, or wherever. I would stay away from cigarettes for long periods of time, and each time I returned to the habit and inhaled I could feel the old scar tissue rip open. Then when I combined smoking with drinking I became miserably ill.

3. There was a pottery shop on the highway near our home in southern California. I'd gone by a hundred times but never stopped. As I lit a cigarette I decided to drive into the pottery shop and have a look around. In my attempt to negotiate a turn into the lot and keep my cigarette from falling into my lap I nicked the fence post and the whole blessed chain link fence went down like a row of dominos. Unbelievable! So, I brought my smoking career to a close.

My dear father-in-law was an excessive smoker. He died of lung cancer. I'd already quit my habit when that shocker occurred. My own father had asthma and claimed smoking opened up his lungs. He developed emphysema, which proved to be the death of him at age 75.

I don't care to get preachy and my smoking friends know I love and care for them while I tolerate their habit. You may want to ask yourself some questions if you're a smoker:

Do you have brown fingers from years of holding lit cigarettes?

Are you ashamed to smile because of yellow teeth?

Is "dragon mouth" or "morning mouth" causing problems with your kissing?

Do non-smokers in your car pool start coughing and open windows when you light up?

Are you tired of emptying ashtrays?

Tired of finding burn holes in your clothes and trying to ignore the marks you've left on the neighbor's coffee table when your cigarette slipped out of the ash tray while you were talking and it burned down too far?

Tired of being tired because of nicotine addiction that has drained your strength and oxygen flow?

Although the greatest percentage of the problem is yours it also involves the innocent bystander. Pollution in your lungs is your choice, but your smoke may be irritating the nose, eyes, throat and allergies of those around you.

Doctors' waiting rooms are off limits for addicted smokers. But some of those people waiting there are exposed to your smoke out there. Maybe they have health problems made worse by your smoke. Perhaps a pregnant woman is struggling with nausea and will have to leave the room to give up her lunch because of your smoking.

Ecologists and smog controllers have begun their work in the formerly smoke-filled rooms of public buildings and businesses. Most of us don't realize we've been so much a part of the smoke and it a part of us. Then we get home and hang up our clothes, and one of the kids politely tells us we stink when we bend over to kiss them good-night and tuck them into their wee-little beds.

Everyone's lungs deserve a break. Especially little children whose parents smoke and fill their kids' little lungs with smoke.

The amazing Vitamin E

When I lived in the smoggy San Gabriel Valley southeast of Los Angeles, my doctor was convinced that I had emphysema. I couldn't blow up a balloon and my breathing registered below its normal capacity. I was heavily into treatment and reconciled to a lifetime of going downhill.

I suffered through the first summer after our move to Oregon. We now had a two-story house. And although I loved the extra space, I had to calculate every trip up and down those stairs because of shortness of breath and a bad case of the "slows."

The University of Oregon Medical School had an emphysema research and testing lab. After a thorough examination they determined "no permanent lung damage." Although the cause of my symptoms was evasive they said it didn't appear that I had emphysema. Great! They recommended I see a cardiac specialist for further study. I kept the phone number of the specialist on hand for the time when I would be so miserable that I would be forced to see another doctor. Like most people I shy away from doctors' offices.

Somewhere along the line I read about Vitamin E. Perhaps the subject came up in a conversation with a friend whom I considered a bit gung-ho on nutrition at the time. Anyway, I began to drag so badly and my eyes became so painful and blurred that I was falling asleep at the wheel of the car when I drove the children to school in the morning, or almost any other time when I drove. I admitted to myself that something had to be done soon.

One day while I was driving down the street I'd driven on dozens of times the big, black lettering on the roof of a small house-like building caught my attention. It spelled HEALTH FOODS. "Why not," says I to myself.

As I opened the door of the health food store there was a rack of paperback books directly in front of me. One book had a big letter "E" on the cover and I picked it out for purchase along with a small bottle of the Vitamin E food supplement.

I figured I'd give this stuff a good test and waited until I felt particularly fatigued. The result of the first 100 units of Vitamin E was amazing. Within the first half-hour my eyes cleared and I started reading the book to find out what had happened. This was the beginning of my road to recovery.

Every body is different. For some reason we think we can all add the same foods together and consume them with the same results. I began to study the needs of my own particular body's action-reaction patterns and over the many years have found combinations of foods and vitamin supplements that maintain this body in reasonably better health than I'd known for years before.

Vitamin E is often referred to as the fertility vitamin, with some advertisements boasting an improvement in sex life. I think Vitamin E has done amazing things for me, but most important, the improvement of my over-all health—along with some common sense rest and diet routines, and periodic checkups with my doctor. I believe that better sexual relationship is a result of better mental and physical health, and no single vitamin should be expected to do everything for every body.

*   *   *

During the pediatrician's examination of my eight year old, he asked, "Do you have any nose trouble?" She answered that she did have a stuffy nose at times. The doctor told me he thought she had an allergy problem and turned to my daughter and asked, "You know what the allergy salute is, don't you?" As she shook her head in the negative he proceeded to demonstrate with a motion pushing up his nose with the palm of his hand, followed by a swift wipe under the nose with the index finger in a horizontal position.

"Now!" he said, "Are you allergic to any certain thing at any certain time?"

"Yes, I'm most allergic in school," she answered with great haste.

Ode to a hamburger

Be ye thick or be ye thin. Be ye medium, rare or well done. Even if we do not love you—we need you.

Never a week passes that we can resist you at the neighborhood grocery store in the meat case. We're helpless when we feel those pangs of hunger while driving and we see your signs begging us to come in and eat.

You present a challenge. How many ways can we disguise hamburger and bring it to our dinner tables? Though we have recipes for over 100 ways to prepare ground beef we regret to say we only use a few. We promise more variety in the future. We promise to read our cookbooks at least once a month.

Children love you. When they go into a restaurant with us they search for your name on the menu. You are familiar and satisfying to them. You represent security.

Old folks love you too. When it's difficult to chew, you and oatmeal become their favorites. You fill a place near our hearts, and though you often cause us heartburn or lack the nourishment we expect, you are a habit.

Lovers munch together over you. Sports fans cheer over you. Dogs bark and beg for you.

When you're ground and gristly you rest comfortably between two halves of a bun, with a pickle, mustard and mayonnaise for dressing. When you're very lean we display you proudly on a plate like a steak.

They may broil or boil you. They may bake or grill you. Even if you are all mixed up with noodles and gravy or long-thin spaghetti and tomato sauce—we will still recognize you.

We realize we've taken you for granted and expect you to fulfill our hungering needs. Though we'd like to leave you alone—we can't.

When we need a meal in a hurry—you're there.

When we pinch pennies at the market—you're there.

You're dependable.

We can't ignore you because you're an in-ground part of our American way-of-life.

How to remove a B-B from a boy's ear

Paul was seven and had a stomachache when it was time to get ready for church. He stayed home in bed with an older sister baby-sitting, and he recovered miraculously when we returned. His plan backfired when I told him he had to take a nap in the afternoon because he was ill.

A few minutes after he went down for his nap he came upstairs and told me, "A B-B slipped into my ear."

"How in the world could a B-B slip into your ear?" I demanded, already knowing the answer. I remembered the cries of pain from other children in our household when tissue was stuffed into the nose and was retrieved in the doctor's office.

"Go ask your father to get it out for you," I said. I knew the situation required calm and poise, but I really wanted to laugh because it seemed so ridiculous.

Most homes have little magnets sort of drifting about. One of the children remembered seeing a magnet that had been removed from the plastic heat deflector for the floor register. Paul's father put the small magnet in his ear and I heard the click for contact. Simple as that if you ever need to remove a B-B from a small boy's ear.

Children become fascinated with their ears and noses at various stages and ages. Sometimes they don't have anything better to do than see how much toilet tissue they can stuff in one small nose.

The unbelievable list of items that small children can put in their mouths and swallow would fill a volume. One time I called the doctor's office when a wee one swallowed a dime, and I asked what to do. The nurse said not to worry because it would pass through the body in a day or two. As a second thought she asked, "Why, do you need the dime?"

*   *   *

When a cigarette commercial appeared on television several years ago my children showed the effects of the counter commercial by speaking up one after the other.

"I don't want to get lung cancer."

I'm not going to smoke when I grow up."

I'm going to smoke when I grow up," said the five-year-old. "Then I can take Nicoban."

Sunflower seeds for health nuts

My children consume great numbers of sunflower seeds. For many years it has been a source of irritation and agitation for me to discover the little piles of hulls about the house when they've finished munching and sucking out all the salt.

I had the children with me at the beach for two weeks during one summer while I attended writing classes. I had already warned them not to leave their little piles of hulls around the beach house. When I returned at noon, it was evident the children had been sunflower seeding in front of the television. Little piles on all the chair and sofa arms.

"Oh no," I simmered, "clean it up before I get back from lunch."

I cooled my temper over a bowl of hot clam chowder and studied the seagulls searching for their lunch on the beach. Every living thing has to eat, but why sunflower seeds?

"Ha, all cleaned up I see," I smiled and agreed to help them get some lunch together. Surely there was an area of compromise in this whole sunflower seed issue.

Later that afternoon I visited the health food store operated by a couple of counter-culture young people. I asked the young man building shelves what he knew about sunflower seeds.

"All I know is that it takes more energy getting them out of the shells than you gain in eating them."

I began my research at the rotating bookrack next to the grain bins. My previous knowledge consisted of viewing the rapid growth of the monster plants behind the garage when I was a kid. It was an interesting plant that hid the peeling paint on the garage and probably chased crows away from the garden.

Aside from being the Kansas State flower, I discovered that the sunflower has been used as an effective medicinal remedy. It can be made into flour for baking, and the oil can be used for soap, candles, and as a lubricant.

The Helianthus Annus (or Sunflower Annual) is also called the Marigold of Peru. The seed is 55 percent protein, 35 percent natural fats, and 100 percent digestible. It is a rich source for the Vitamin B grouping, and is used as a meat substitute in some cases because it contains more protein than meat, eggs or cheese.

The Zuni Indians mixed the roots of the sunflower with two other herbs to treat rattlesnake bite. The Aztec Indians revered the sunflower and had its symbol in gold in their temples. The Thompson Indians of British Columbia had a *Prayer to the Sunflower*, which says in part, "Mayest thou always help me to ascend, so that I may always reach the top of the mountain, and may never be clumsy . . . "

The sunflower is an excellent compost soil fortifier.

I gradually withdrew my objections to the sunflower seed. As a peace offering I purchased a pound of hull-less seeds for the children.

The next day the children went to the store and again purchased their little sacks of sunflower seeds. I returned from class to see the little piles of hulls, and the seeds that I'd purchased still sitting, unopened, on the kitchen cupboard.

"What goes?" I collapsed into a chair and viewed the hulls scattered on the floor, in ashtrays, between the cushions of the couch.

"We like the salt," Teresa said as she spat another soggy shell into an ashtray.

For all the nutritional value in the sunflower seed they still wanted the struggle of getting it out of the hull. They actually get their kicks from removing the salt, cracking the hull between their teeth, munching on the seed and spitting out the remainder. They have it down to a science.

They haven't quit leaving soggy piles of hulls around and I haven't stopped complaining. Maybe my complaining is also part of the enjoyment they get from eating sunflower seeds. I'm reasonably content that it's not candy wrappers they're piling up.

My experience with hypnosis in childbirth

Hypnosis: a valuable tool or a dangerous weapon?

I don't intent to reach any scientific conclusions regarding hypnosis, but perhaps I can shed a little light.

Hypnosis has different meanings for different people. For the medical profession it can be defined in part as, "a temporary condition of altered attention in the subject which may be induced by another person and in which a variety of phenomena may appear spontaneously or in response to verbal or other stimuli . . . "

According to one of my psychology instructors, hypnosis is a state of heightened suggestibility" and the World Book Encyclopedia says it's a state of "increased susceptibility to suggestion."

Is it theatrics or anesthesia? Each of us can be influenced by some personal experience or gained knowledge. Personally I've always been repelled by the display of stage show hypnosis—and impressed by the potential and real value of hypnosis as an anesthetic.

My third child was delivered in a breach position. I've since come to realize how traumatic and dangerous that kind of delivery can be for the child, and the mother. I wept when I saw her bruised buttocks from the hard laboring effort to exit. Naturally I experienced some emotional and physical trauma. I became a guinea pig for the tranquilizer industry. My mother-in-law, God love her, was a rock of support during those days. She was a mother who understood me, and she often cared for the children to give me a break. My own mother was thousands of miles across the country and offered moral support.

Then I became pregnant for our fourth child. My body was saying, "Oh, God, no!" and the highest part of my intellect said, "I accept." I already was undergoing treatment for a stomach ulcer and heart irregularity—and life was depressing. But, down deep, or up high, I knew we'd make it. The child I carried helped pull me back to the land of the living.

My obstetrician was one of those rare individuals who related in a very human way and didn't tell me that my mental anguish was "all in your head." For reasons known only to him, he suggested that we use hypnosis in lieu of any other anesthetic when delivery time came. I was a skeptic but agreed because I hoped it might work for me.

I consulted a priest regarding the ethics of using hypnosis and he assured me I'd be in competent hands and that hypnosis is a valid medical tool.

Sessions for developing the post hypnotic suggestion can be time consuming and perhaps this is one reason it is in limited use in the medical profession. I had four of the 15-minute training or suggestibility sessions before labor began, and one more before delivery.

Hypnosis became less mysterious. Relaxation was the key to success. I began to reason that if the hypnosis didn't eliminate the pain then at least I would have enjoyed the preparation. I was never in a deep sleep or trance, always aware and relaxed.

I had to listen carefully to the soft voice speaking to me from behind the desk with only the desk light on in the darkened office. I had to shut out all distracting sounds. I felt that I could break the "spell" anytime I wanted. The doctor told me I could. I was in total control.

The doctor told me I would experience pressure without pain when labor began. I was concerned about the heart irregularities and at one time I had convinced myself I would die from the strain of childbirth. But I was so noble that it would be worth the sacrifice. My concerns gradually disappeared. Everyone knows there's nothing better for the heart than relaxation and stress reduction.

I had just finished hanging a new set of drapes in my living room the day labor began. I was particularly upset with the drapes because they had miscalculated and the drapes didn't cover the windows. Nevertheless, I knew I couldn't do any more about it that day. I had to get ready for an appointment with the doctor that afternoon.

I felt pressure in the abdomen and pelvic area. I ignored it and did the family wash, arranged for a sitter to come in, packed my traveling bag, and drove myself to the doctor's office.

My visit to the doctor's office confirmed my suspicions that I was in advanced labor. The hospital was just around the corner and the doctor advised me to go there immediately and he would be right over. I debated with myself as I drove around the block. I really thought I should go home and fix supper for my family, but decided to take the doctor's advice. I parked the car, signed myself in at 5:30 p.m. I talked the nurse into letting me out of bed to go down the hall and make a phone call asking my mother-in-law to go over to the house to relieve the sitter and stay with the children. Another phone call to my husband's office informed me he was in route.

Although I was functioning under the post-hypnotic suggestion

I was wide awake and feeling no pain, extremely alert. The delivery was an enjoyable experience. I viewed the delivery with the aid of well-positioned mirrors, and a daughter was born 35 minutes after I had signed myself in at the hospital.

For some strange reason hypnosis didn't work with the after-pains. It has been my experience that each additional baby increased the pain after birth when the uterus contracts back to normal. Such is life. Can't have everything, I guess.

Hypnosis helped me to experience painless, joyful childbirth. In the right hands, hypnosis is a valuable and amazing tool. It has been used in surgery as well as in childbirth. It has aided the mentally ill. It has also been useful in dentistry.

Hypnosis isn't a toy to be played with by amateurs. It could turn into a dangerous weapon if a person submits his will and trusts the suggestions of the wrong people.

Working my way through college

"It's not true, Lincoln did not free the slaves," I mumbled the complaint as I crawled into bed at three in the morning.

That was the first night of the first week of two long summer months working as a broccoli trimmer on the swing shift at the cannery. I had not yet benefited from the valuable experience and interesting people that would come into my life.

What does a middle-class, middle-age suburban homemaker, writer learn by breaking out of a comfortable mold and creeping into a whole other life style?

The body adapts.

I smelled the broccoli blocks away. I wondered how I could ever stand it for the season. On the inside it was bound to be worse. After the first week, I stopped holding my breath when passing the blanching machines with their steaming, hot broccoli bouncing over the belts.

My weak wrist and bursitis-ridden shoulder couldn't possibly make it. But they did, and I did. Ben-gay, eye drops and vitamins got me through the first week, plus an occasional tablet for nausea.

"Your body adjusts," said my friend Margie who was trimming for the fourth season and convinced me it was a good way to earn the college tuition, "you can make it if you really want to."

It was the "want to" that gave me trouble. The first paycheck helped some. And since I already had four days in on the next paycheck by that time it kept me going "just a few more days."

A few more days, a day at a time, got me through the season and lost me most of my summer. I was earning my way through college and believed it was worth the effort. Meanwhile I was getting on-the-job training about people. During lunch breaks and when working on the line I tried to learn something about where they were coming from.

The second to the last night I worked before going back to school, I suddenly stopped trimming broccoli and stared out at the mass of people across the huge warehouse filled with rumbling, screeching machinery. There were many shades of green in the big boxes, on the belts and on the floor. I wondered how much I had learned.

From a self-proclaimed "hippie" I learned how to beat the system by becoming a victim.

"In this country the productive people are penalized by high taxes," said the clean-shaven young man in plaid shirt and blue jeans. "I had a paint contracting business in California. Earning money like mad—but loosing my shirt in taxes and expenses. Figured out it wasn't worth it."

Now he's on food stamps. Doesn't work long enough to earn the right to pay taxes. Has money stashed away in Canadian banks earning over nine percent interest (1970s), and is financially ready for the "coming crash."

That same young man received a college education while residing in a California prison on a drug pushing charge. While he was working at the cannery he earned extra money by buying short and selling long. Someone had an old car and they needed money in a hurry, "the hippie" was there with the cash. The IRS was ignored in the transaction that was never recorded for posterity.

One night I was trimming next to a young woman I remembered

from a psychology class we both attended. I remembered how intelligent she appeared when she answered or asked questions during the term. Now, she had enough academics and believed "you only benefit from life's experiences." She had been receiving welfare money to support herself and a young son but she felt guilty about taking a public dole. She was working swing shift until she saved enough money to go to Mexico where they both could "live better for less."

A middle-age housewife needed a freezer, and quit when she earned enough for that. A shy, curly-hair teenager with a heavily acne-scarred face was working two jobs to pay the hospital bills resulting from a car accident when his auto rolled over half a dozen times on an icy Portland street during the winter. His insurance paid $6,000 of the $10,000 hospital bill and he had more than $2,000 yet to be paid on the loan.

A slim, intense dark-haired woman with two growing boys works two jobs in food processing plants because her husband had been out of work for several months and the bills piled up. Sometime in the few remaining hours she slept.

Seasonal work is often a family affair, with mother, father and older children all drawing a paycheck. There were several of these combinations among the Mexican-Americans. I tried to learn something about the language and people. I came to know and love many of them. One elderly Hispanic lady trimmed next to me several times and tried to teach me some conversational Spanish. She spoke very broken English and we fought the deafening noises from the machines for our brief lessons.

At one point in my career as a common laborer an acquaintance of mine asked, "How does it feel to be out among the low-income people?" I bristled with resentment.

"You know nothing about the people who work there," I shot back, "just as I knew nothing when I started. There are all kinds of people and I don't look down on any of them. At least they're working hard to earn honest money."

The once distasteful surroundings blended into a backdrop for the people who acted out their parts in life at the cannery each dusk to dawn. The red, white, blue, yellow, green and orange hard-hats of the management and other personnel drifted in and out of the picture of hair-netted women and blue-capped men. Everyone was involved in the business of moving tons of broccoli from one end of the huge building to the other, and off to the public.

I spent over an hour scraping and cleaning broccoli out of the grooves on the bottom of my waffle-stomper shoes at the end of my working season. Shoes that I had parked in the garage each night along with the car because they stank from broccoli. Shoes that had waded through the green broccoli scraps that had fallen at my feet as I raced with the clock each hour to meet my quota. Shoes that could have belonged to someone else at some other time—but I walked and worked in them, and learned to know about and care for the uncommon laborer.

Coping when money's tight

My father's salary was a carefully guarded secret at our house. So I never knew if we were poor. I guess being poor means—compared to something else. Compared to most people I knew we had about the same.

It's a popular sport among us older folk to point out how little we had and how much more the kids today have. It seems to me it wasn't so much what we had or lacked, but rather our attitude about the matter. We were great compensators. In the first place we didn't ask for much. We may have stood at the store window and drooled a bit, but somewhere down deep we knew we shouldn't ask.

When I was in the first grade all the kids took their pennies to school to buy candy after lunch. Usually Mom gave me a penny or two without asking. Sometimes we both forgot on purpose. Once I asked, even though I knew it was embarrassing for her to be without the pennies I asked for. Then she dug into the cedar chest that had been her "hope chest" before she married Dad. The chest was filled with interesting items, like coins and jeweled stickpins for ties, old greeting cards and other keepsakes. She produced an

Indian head dime and put it into my small hand. I felt guilty spending the coin from that precious collection. Years later I understood its real value.

It's bad enough being without, but it's worse when people tell you about it. All along you think life is good. Then you get to high school and a girlfriend can't come to your house because it's on the other side of the tracks.

I suppose it's like the mole I once had on my cheek by my right ear—it never bothered me until someone mentioned it. Then I became self-conscious.

When I was growing up we had enough to share with those who had less. People were on welfare—and it hurt. It hurt their pride and dignity because they were people who would have worked if work were to be found.

There have been depressions and recessions. The "great depression" of the late Twenties and early Thirties taught some lessons that could carry individuals and families through their personal financial depression or national economic recession.

Some historical accounts of the "great depression" indicate that many people survived and ultimately prospered because they maintained a family unity that nourished warm relationships, organized a pull-together atmosphere, helped those with less and deepened their faith.

Many others fought tooth and nail to dig their way out of poverty to succeed at business and fail at life.

The "great depression" also prompted public and private assistance agencies to aid individuals and families in financial crisis. A look through the phone book and a few phone calls can often relieve pressure and provide valuable information.

Unlike the Thirties, the majority of families in the Seventies struggle to maintain a comfort level rather than a subsistence level. The enjoy-now, pay-later philosophy of economics caught many folks short of change.

Sometimes families pull together in time of financial crisis, but money problems can cause a split as well.

Solutions begin in attitude. The concepts of need and want

became juxtaposed through affluence. Many of those hit by the depression of the Thirties hadn't tasted the luxuries of life and the comedown wasn't quite the adjustment it is today. We were not yet surrounded by the material appeal offered on television, as well as the results of expanding economy, technology and production.

It's difficult to say "No!" to a child who sees his neighbor friend with a new bike, or an entertainment center in his bedroom. Big items are easier to handle than the little day-to-day "No!" that has to be dished out with regularity.

Rather than lecture the differences between need and want it helps to post a sheet of paper in a convenient spot (the refrigerator door seems best around here) with a "NEED" column and a "WANT" column. Dangle a pencil from a string and let each family member determine what it is they need or want.

This method of dividing the spoils can accomplish two things. First, they will be making the judgments themselves and not having it inflicted upon them. Also, it will waylay some of the verbal pressure that often overwhelms moms and dads.

"Hey, Mom! I need a new pair of blue jeans" is often lost in the deluge of "I need a dozen cookies for the Blue Birds" or "I need a new battery for my Walkman radio."

Individual family members examine needs and wants based on what they know to be a tight money situation. If the family has a budget for spur of the moment "need" items it might help to post that amount for viewing. Older children can do simple math and decide where individual needs fit in.

Wishing and wanting are inevitable. People have a right to their dreams—even material dreams. Sometimes today's dreams give way to tomorrow's realities, and they change. A real need has to be dealt with on its own terms. A new bike *can be earned*. It's not impossible. But responsibility for its attainment must often be shared, or in some cases assumed entirely by the one with the dream that has become the need.

Don't try to keep up with the neighbors. Maybe they can afford their new car and swimming pool, and maybe they're deep in debt. They have a different income, different situation and an entirely different set of priorities.

Don't panic. Try to keep everything in perspective. Realize what you can and can't do to change your situation. Maybe it's practical for mother to work temporarily—and then again maybe you'll end up paying more in taxes, and for childcare, clothing and transportation than it's worth.

When the budgets are tight there are generally two directions to go, either bring in more money or reduce spending. A third alternative may be a carefully thought out plan of shifting emphasis on how much money goes into different areas of non-fixed expenses.

Don't nag, or point accusing fingers. Maybe income hasn't kept up with outgo. Maybe it's the fault of one mate or the other. Maybe it's the unhappy result of not being able to adjust rapidly enough in a runaway inflation or recession period. It's a time for building each other up rather than tearing down. Time for cooperation not competition.

Don't waste valuable time on unproductive worry. Sometimes it seems like you'll have to live this way the rest of your life, but life happens one day at a time, and progress often is slow.

Negative thoughts can cut you off at the knees. You don't have to look hard or far to find someone in worse condition. Reaching out to another—even in a small way—can help change our attitude toward facing tomorrow.

Negative thoughts are contagious and spread through families like flu in winter.

There's nothing funny about juggling income with outgo the first of the month, or buying inferior brands at the grocery store. A "Laugh or Perish" sign should be posted in bold over the most used doorways in the house. Without a sense of humor and the ability to chuckle over a chuck roast when you wish it was a top sirloin, all may be lost. A smile often turns the tide of attitude for the better.

If the family economics' charts say you should be spending $200 a week to feed a family of four moderately, well don't get discouraged if you're spending less. You probably know something the chart makers don't know and wish they did. You've probably made considerable adjustments in purchasing, preparing and complaining. Probably back to the basics and nobody's starving.

We try to tell ourselves that money isn't everything. There are other important things in life that deserve our attention. Too often when money's tight that's all we can think about, and it saps our enthusiasm for all the "best things in life that are free."

Patience becomes more than a virtue, it's a survival tool.

Easy money hard to find

Many years ago when we were living in the Los Angeles area I bought a raffle ticket from a friend to help out her church. Early one Sunday morning she called and said I'd won the first prize of $125. (In those days that was a lot of money.) So, I dropped an extra couple of bucks in the Sunday collection that day and told my husband I'd take him to Las Vegas the following weekend. Easy come and easy go for once in my life. Ordinarily I hold on to money with a Scottish grip.

Another time, my parents visited us in Los Angeles and we drove them over to Las Vegas for a treat. Dad played the silver dollar slot machine with complete abandon and suddenly an avalanche of silver poured out and the lights flashed and bells rang. Mother started scooping up the silver dollars in one of those nice little buckets they give you for your loose change.

The prize for that machine was $100. The man in the cage took the bucket of silver dollars and put a crisp $100 greenback on the counter next to a single silver dollar that represented Dad's original investment. Mother picked up the greenback, folded it neatly and tucked it safely away, and gave Dad his silver dollar.

I've found that in betting at the races the only difference between the horses and the dogs is size. I come home with about the same amount of change in my pocket, regardless of which animal races.

There was one time when I took a psychology class and the instructor experimented with statistical analysis and concentration.

We flipped coins, rolled dice, and four women students lifted a husky football player using two fingers each and concentration.

These ESP (extra sensory perception) experiments built up my courage. I would try it on the dogs at the races. After all, I had come out on top of the ESP test in class that day—and I had confidence in me.

When my husband read the evening paper after dinner I stood over him and said, "Would you like to go somewhere tonight or do you want to stay home and watch television?"

"Where do you want to go, to the dog races?" He asked.

How about that? His ESP was working, too. So, off we went to the Ladies Night at the dog races and I planned to play the long shots.

I won on two long shots and when I balanced everything out I came home with 80 cents more than when I left. My husband won on a quenelle after I told him to change his way of betting. So he finally came away with $6 to the good. Had we stayed for the last two races we probably would have dropped our winnings easily.

Maybe ESP would have worked better on horses. It was my first dog race and I kept calling the greyhounds "horses." Perhaps the dogs rebelled when they got wind of my foolproof system.

Youths seek job opportunities

There are those fortunate people who don't have to work in order to eat, but I don't know any of them personally. I sometimes think my generation has put too great an emphasis on the acquisition of money and goods. Our kids certainly learned it somewhere.

Everyone moves forward from what they know. I grew up in a modest house that had indoor plumbing and a coal furnace that later was converted to natural gas. The conversion meant that I no longer had to help my mother lift two metal tubs over our heads and out the basement window to be dragged by the handle over the snow to the curb for pick up. On one hand the conversion from coal to gas eliminated some jobs for kids who earned spending money helping neighbors.

My brother and I had a *Liberty* and *Saturday Evening Post* delivery route. Then the magazines took to mail delivery. We raked leaves in the autumn and shoveled snow in the winter. We sang Christmas carols late into the cold nights to get the last of our pennies together to have something to put under the tree for our parents.

When money's tight kids sometimes turn to petty thievery. More than a couple of boys in my neighborhood had seen the inside of a reform school. Along with some of my friends I learned to be quick with my hands and nonchalant in my appearance. We never stole necessity items. No one was starving or sleeping out in the cold. Getting something for nothing and dare-devilishness drove us to lifting candy bars and other nickel and dime items.

My biggest, and last, hoist was a pair of pink and white knitted booties for my doll. I didn't really need them and wasn't even sure at the time they were the right size. I took a dare and joined the club. I never tried them on my doll and they stayed tucked safely away until I went to the priest and confessed all. The hardest penance of all, he said I had to return the doll booties. Have you ever tried to appear nonchalant while returning stolen goods? I trembled with fear of being caught pulling the booties out of my pocket and slipping them into the section partitioned by glass on the counter of the "Dime Store."

I knew then there are two kinds of people. Those who can lie, cheat and steal with aplomb. And there were people like me.

When I turned 16, I went right out looking for a job. I had no experience. Naturally, experience is what everyone wanted. I covered about eight miles, both sides of the street in two cities, on foot. Jobs were scarce in the Detroit suburbs in the late 1940s. One of the stores that showed some interest in my services was a baby clothing store. Naturally, they sold baby booties. Though it had been years between bootie experiences I didn't think I would feel comfortable in that environment. Another option I wasn't too keen about was working in a "Dime Store."

The last place I checked on my long day was a dry cleaning outlet. I stood outside the door and debated with myself because it was getting late and I still had a two-mile walk home. At the point I was ready to give up I pushed open the door and put in my last application for the day. I got a job out of it.

That first real income was dear to me. It made me feel worthwhile because someone was willing to give me money for my services. I liked working, but being paid gave me status, and bought things I wanted and needed.

It's hard to throw stones and accuse the young people today of being materialistic. They didn't invent it.

My children have worked in the strawberry fields as pickers, delivered newspapers, bused tables, cleaned houses, cut grass, watered lawns, fed cats, walked dogs, sat with babies, and even put on spook shows in the garage—to earn money.

When the oldest boy was nearly 12 he and his older sister decided they wanted to go to Disneyland. We moved to Oregon the previous year, and they were restless to return to see friends and relatives in southern California. They both worked for weeks picking berries to pay for their trip. When their Dad took them to the airport to buy their tickets the 12-year-old emptied his pockets. There were tens of dollars in bills and lots of loose change. He held up the line while the clerk carefully counted out the exact amount.

Hearing about it made me wish I had been there, for I believe it would have been one of those rare proud moments when you feel like hugging your kids for being so beautiful. And when the plane took off I'm certain it didn't bother him in the least that his hands were still stained red. He had a summer of rising at 5:00 a.m., catching a bus to ride for miles to the berry field, and picking strawberries in the hot sun or cool drizzle.

Another child paid for a 10-speed bike with berry stained hands, and the oldest girl kept gas in her first car by busing tables. When she came home one day and told me a friend of hers said, "My father wouldn't let me do that kind of work," I nearly orbited. There's no job too menial as long as it's honest work.

There are some rough times when a son or daughter tries so hard to find work and nothing turns up. The discouragement when they get severance notices from an employer. There are times when nothing you can say will help, and all you can do is cry along with them.

Grocery store carryout girls

The high school girl with blond hair tied back into a ponytail and a metallic orthodontic smile boxed and carried my groceries. Only yesterday a young man performed those duties.

I carried groceries when my mother did her Saturday morning shopping. My boys and girls have all been given that chore at one time or another. So, why was I surprised to have a girl carry my groceries and load them into the car? Maybe it was the look on the face of my teenage son as he watched her.

When I questioned a carryout boy on a later trip to the store he informed me that the girl was hired to shame the boys into working harder. She applied for the job, that had something to do with it as well. It beat babysitting money and has since led to her becoming a checkout person.

We're gradually becoming accustomed to girls doing jobs formerly performed by boys, but we're still a long way from a real adjustment in attitude toward women in the work force. Maybe someday a woman can be an auto mechanic and a man can be a secretary without disturbing the equilibrium. Not many men will rush out to seek jobs as file clerks, stenographers or secretaries until the pay goes up.

More women are working and raising families. More women have entered higher-paying positions, and in some cases becoming a threat to males. It's not just a matter of ego, but primarily a matter of economics. In some fields, men are losing out to women who have increased their skills and are advancing.

There are too many options open to women. So many ways they can go with their lives. It's difficult to know how to guide the young girls. If women are encouraged to pursue careers they really love, will they also have the same opportunity and equal pay as men in their field of endeavor?

Even though women may achieve an equal-pay-for-equal-work status there are centuries of attitudes that may never change. There are times, in the quiet of our hearts, when we wonder how much change we really can handle.

Automobile: most dangerous weapon in the U.S.A.

With fear and trembling hidden behind a frozen smile, I place the car keys in the hands of another teenager and slide prayerfully into the passenger seat and buckle up.

At this writing I've played the above scene four times and have four more to go. As I grow older and grayer, I don't think I've gotten any better at relaxing during those trial runs during the driver permit days. Sometimes self pity gets the better of me and I think, "Haven't I suffered enough?"

My own teenage driving career was nipped in the bud when I tried to maneuver the family car around a corner. My own dear Mother screamed as I struggled with the split second decision to press the gas pedal rather than the brake or clutch. It was a poor choice. No harm done as the car was brought quickly under control and Mother and I exchanged places. That was the last time I got my hands on the steering wheel of the family car until I was married, 22 years old and had a daughter of my own.

I remember that I cried bitter tears at the age of 17 going on 18 when I begged to buy the family car as they planned to buy another. It was humiliating for me to have to depend on someone else for a ride, or to walk, or take a bus.

Competent persons shouldn't have to wait until age 20 to get a driver's license. Nor is it required that children go to the motor vehicle department at the age of 15 to get their permits, or take the road test the day they turn 16. Without a doubt, the car conflicts between teenagers and their parents are among some of the most painful encounters in those years between childhood and adulthood that we call adolescence.

Our three oldest children have each owned their own cars in their senior year of high school. This is about the time they were working at part time jobs long enough to put away a few dollars for the purchase of a used car and insurance. Then they are on the work-car treadmill. They need a car to get to work and they need a job to keep up the car.

They become committed to mobility just like the rest of us and their cars become the second major item they'll acquire in their lifetime. They begin to realize the difference between a bike and a car is more than the size and price of tires.

Our generous "Uncle"

Uncle Gimme is giving away money today. In fact, every day is give-money-away day in the U.S.A.

An uncle to us all and as generous as he can be. If you don't succeed in having your fondest wishes granted upon the first request for funding—then try, try again.

I've been told that there's no end in sight, no bottom to the barrel of money into which Uncle reaches.

There's a strange correlation between the amount of money that Uncle has to spend each year and the increase in the number of dollars that go out of pocket in taxes—somebody's pocket.

So many worthy causes and so many tremendous expenses that a good uncle wouldn't want to play favorites—everyone gets their share. And if there hasn't been an established program to get the funds then Uncle will just make the money available to the one who comes up with the best way to use the funds.

I don't mean to sound sarcastic, but it would seem that some people are asking for what they are getting—or is it, getting what they are asking for?

"It is happily announced that federal funds are available for our project. A grant, a loan, a subsidy—oh happy day!"

I grew up with the impression that someone pays the bills. Uncle is retired and without visible means of support, so where else would he go but to his immediate family for the necessary dollars to continue his benevolence?

In many cases Uncle is able to do things for us that we cannot do for ourselves. But, ever since we, the public turned our individual backs on the poor, Uncle has had to help them collectively. They saw us being comfortable in our homes and they wanted to be fed, clothed and housed, as well.

We take great national pride in watching our astronauts land on the Moon or on Mars, but the financing of the project doesn't come out of the atmosphere. We're supposed to look the other way when all these big items appear in the budget—and leave it all to Uncle.

Everyone knows the cost of defense is up, and not likely to come down. There's not much sense in blaming the present President when he had plenty of help from his predecessors in complicating the situation. No one has all the answers, but everyone in the world thinks the United States has all the money, all the resources, and all the manpower.

The national debt is going out of sight again, and I can't imagine what a billion dollars looks like, or imagine multiplying that billion by hundreds more.

We've suffered through inflationary periods where our standard of living was raised to a level not likely to be achieved anywhere else in the world. We enjoy our creature comforts, and a goodly amount of freedom.

As a nation we can produce instant demand—all you have to do is show us something we haven't got.

Happiness is . . .

Happiness is a state of mind that tells us we are progressing toward a worthwhile goal.

Happiness rests in the memory and in the imagination.

Happiness is quiet exhalation in the awareness of existence.

Seams of world laced with happiness

"Peace on earth, good will to men." Or is it "to men of good will?"

The first phrase is unconditional and the second is conditional. Somewhere during the years of Christmas card printing the phrase has been altered. Both are good, the second is more nearly correct.

To everyone, I extend the first greeting of "peace on earth, good will to men." And hopefully, as a result of becoming more peaceful their wills will be directed toward more good.

To those who already feel they are aimed in the right direction I extend the second greeting of "peace on earth to men of good will."

How can something as simple as a Christmas greeting on the inside of a card be so complicated, or why should it be complicated? Perhaps we never read the greetings anyway. Open the card to identify the sender, scan the print, glance at the graphics, and sigh with relief if we've sent the sender a greeting.

A small word like "peace" requires contemplation for understanding. For those who have never known peace the word may fall on deaf ears. For those who can recall brief encounters with peaceful moments a new search may begin.

"Peace" like "love" carries its special meaning to each person so why bother to define the term on a card. Let the receiver believe that the sender knew exactly what they both meant.

I wish you peace—an absence of war. A time when families are together and there is no fighting there, or on other battlefields.

I wish that people would stop killing one another with weapons and words, either slowly or quickly, at home or abroad. I wish it were true that women rulers could eliminate war, for we'd surely consent to being ruled by the weaker sex. But territorial gains know no barriers for men or women.

The United States attempted a universal "peacekeeping effort" in Korea and Vietnam to the point of foolishness, and still the world refuses to lay down its arms. To lay down arms without a better weapon would be foolish, and the search for an adequate replacement goes on and on.

I wish you peace—the absence of quarrels and disagreements. So that harmony may rule wherever two or more are gathered together—rather than riots. So many people search for some kind of serenity, but they give up when patience runs out.

So many suffer the absence of the spiritual necessities of life— the true coping and survival tools.

I wish you peace—peace of mind, because, without it there can be no happiness. And we need happy people to keep the seams of the world from ripping out completely.

VI

PREACHING WHAT WE PRACTICE

All the good intentions, beautiful philosophies and vivid dreams are of little use to us or to anyone else unless they are expressed in some kind of action. I hesitate to hold an unyielding attitude toward my own principles. I hardly ever say "never" anymore. For nothing is so indigestible as the words I've uttered in a moment of pomp and been forced to eat in a flurry of circumstances.

Listen to the children

"There are those who believe something, and therefore will tolerate nothing; and on the other hand, those who tolerate everything, because they believe nothing."—Robert Browning

And somewhere between there is a happy medium. I can't imagine anything more necessary than staying somewhere toward the middle of that road during these days of intensive pressures from all directions.

When I was growing up the adults didn't talk much about religion and politics in polite company, to prevent straining the level of their tolerance and the extent of their friendships. Gradually these barriers have been dropped and any subject is fair game.

Learning a fair degree of tolerance is a stretch and growth process. If we didn't occasionally feel irritation and anger over the words and actions of others we would never realize our level of tolerance. Every day offers many challenges in this regard.

I have to admit that going back to college and associating with people half my age taught me a degree of tolerance I would not have otherwise learned. In turn, many of them learned to tolerate me, and some of my expressed views.

In looking beyond the opinions of other students I discovered persons willing to exchange ideas. I work on being a good listener. This is not a fault reserved for one generation—both need practice in listening.

It is an easy matter to learn to tolerate others compared to the task of allowing persons in our own household to be different from us.

Without knowing it we try to mold our children into our image and likeness as though we were the living example of everything a person should be. If they were just like us we probably would learn to hate them rather quickly.

One evening when I returned from a meeting, one of the girls surprised me by cleaning the kitchen in an unbelievable manner. I was immediately struck by her efficiency and told her as much.

And then I remembered, I used to hate it when my mother would nag at me to get a job done. I would say, "If you'll just leave me alone I'll get it done."

When she went out for an afternoon or evening I'd get busy at some task that I hadn't been told to do because I wanted her to be surprised.

The fact is, I was doing with my children the same thing I hated so much as a child. I learned something I hope sticks with me longer than a week.

It's important to listen to the children. It's also important to put yourself in their shoes for a time and listen to yourself. It's amazing when we hear our children parrot our phrases or actions, and then we have to discipline them for it.

I think, at times, our children are more like us than we care to admit. One of my favorite pieces of writing is hanging on the wall in most of the offices of children's doctors, "The Art of Parenthood" by Wilferd A. Peterson. One line states, "When we practice tolerance they will be tolerant."

With more years of experience behind us it would be reasonable to expect parents to take a more tolerant attitude toward their children. And to quote George Elliot, "The responsibility of tolerance lies with those who have the wider vision."

*   *   *

Tina, age 7, said, "I'm going to run away from home."
"Wait, I'll go with you," said I.
"I want to run away from you," said Tina.

Slogans for survival

I don't have a sign on my desk that says "SMILE" or "THINK," But here and there when I open a cupboard door there is a message inside.

At some time in my life I started leaving little inspirational messages about the house so that when I discovered them I would take time to think. They also may be termed "mood changer."

I imagine that most people have these little "mood changers" scattered about their lives. New ones replace the old, and old ones sometimes become so friendly that they stay.

On the cork board above my typewriter I have a variety of messages to myself. A favorite one-liner I copied from a book on novel writing reads, "You can't edit what you haven't written." In bold black on white, this message reminds me often that I'm way behind and had better catch up.

For reasons unknown to myself, I have posted the green paper with my 50 cent handwriting analysis from the state fair. It says, "You are conservative by nature. You are able to overcome temperamental periods. You have a retentive memory for important facts. You are sympathetic, and a good listener. The use of psychology comes natural to you."

I'll bet there are 20,000 people out there who have received the identical analysis. I keep it as a morale booster for those days when I feel stupid and inadequate.

Hanging below the handwriting analysis is my most recent letter of acceptance from a Canadian magazine for an article they intend to publish. Then, next to that I have posted the "20 rules for good writing" and the "Art of Parenthood" by Wilferd Peterson.

Before anyone gets the impression that I spend all my time in the laundry room at the typewriter let me tell you of a few "mood changer" I have in the kitchen.

A favorite "mood changers" was cut off a large calendar several years ago. It is a picture of the "Busy Mother" with her 19 children climbing all over her and oozing out of a shoe house. My children have drawn beards and mustaches on some of the faces over the years, but there it remains, for all to see, on the inside of the kitchen door leading to the garage.

Below the "Busy Mother" (who helps me to keep from feeling sorry for myself) there is a poem titled "Happiness" by William George Jordan. And I have a favorite line from that poem that reads, "Man is the creator of his own happiness, it is the aroma of a life lived in harmony with high ideals."

Over my kitchen sink on the inside of a cupboard door I have "A Parent's Prayer." I sometimes think of that as my crying corner. When I get terribly frustrated I read one particular line that gets me back on the track. "Give me courage to say 'NO' to them when I should, regardless of their pleading and temporary sadness."

Inside the door by the phone I have a practical item called "American druggist counter doses for the home." In case of an emergency it calms me down while I read through the list of possible poisons and antidotes, then decide the best thing to do is get the kid to throw up as soon as possible.

One of my more recent inside-cupboard-door additions is back down in the laundry room over my desk. I have had this message posted in long hand for a couple of years and just got around to typing it into more readable form. It is the secret of success. It is a message I gleaned from a recording by Earl Nightengale on the subject of "success." It's one of the best "mood changers" I have. It lists several rules for creating the kind of self-image that will, in time, achieve certain self-determined goals.

And the message I have pinned to the outside of my laundry room door is meant to change the mood of those who enter, "Quiet! Genius at work."

Snowy days and school closures

The snow came, it drifted, froze, and then washed away with the rain. We had heat and we had light through it all. A friend called one night to tell me of their plight, no heat or light for a whole day. Another friend put in a wood-burning stove during the second day without heat or light.

When I heard about these two cases I told my kids to quit complaining about the powdered skim milk they were forced to drink for three days I couldn't get to the store. The mailman looked a bit bedraggled making his appointed rounds, just missing one day's delivery. We still haven't seen the men who pick up the trash. We finally burned 75 percent of the collected rubbish in the fireplace with a roaring good fire that drove most of the family downstairs.

Just when it looked like the Christmas vacation was over, and five of the children would return to school, my oldest daughter got the word from a friend via telephone that St. Mary of the Valley Academy would not resume classes on schedule. I have four very pleased and excited girls with an extra week of vacation because of transportation problems and illness among the nuns at school.

Just to reassure myself that it wasn't all a mistake, I called the school. Sister said many of the nuns were recuperating from the flu and didn't have their full strength yet. So, because of the transportation problems (because the bus must travel great distances into the countryside) and illness—school would wait a few days or a week longer.

Oh, happy day!

How could anything so beautiful cause so much misery? It was the biggest news in town—snow. And after five days of "cabin fever" it seems fair to assume that children and snow go together.

"It's sticking!" Those were the words that brought my children's noses pressing against the windows.

I have a two and a four year old that I haven't been able to get out of the house for weeks, but when the snow covered the ground they could no longer be restrained. On with the boots and mittens—off with the boots and mittens. Everyone had his own heat register to dry snow paraphernalia until I discovered it was more efficient to throw everything into the clothes dryer and make them wear their clothes a second time before washing.

We have one neighbor who drew the envy of all with his "Skee Doo" (plus caboose) by taking his children and their friends up and down the streets. When the snow packed down real good the teenage crowd took the sleds out under the street lights. One boy even donned his skis and went sailing by the house a few times.

After this column appeared in the paper one of my readers wrote me to "quit your whining and enjoy nature's gift." So, I did.

Putting the world in its place

I was unfashionably early for the meeting. People already were seated in the front of the room. I slipped quietly into a back row, picked up the sheet of paper laying on the chair. The paper rattled, heads turned and my face felt warm and red. I smiled and sat down. Unaccustomed as I was to being early, I wasn't sure I was in the right place.

I began to look around the room for familiar faces and for something in the new faces to set me at ease, but the faces were turned toward each other. Mouths were moving but I was too far away to hear.

Maybe I didn't belong!

How often do we enter new rooms or new experiences and have that gnawing feeling of not belonging? The above situation is hypothetical. Not that I haven't felt that way on occasion.

There are places we go where we want people to think we have been there before, to think we belong. How often will a stranger ask us a question about the place where we happen to be and we know nothing? Perhaps we look like we belong and are familiar with our surroundings. And how often have we asked others when they also were new?

I have attended meetings where the content was hazy because the atmosphere in the meeting room was so unfriendly. Then there are those who say we bring our unfriendliness with us. It becomes especially difficult when everyone else appears to know one another. They have something to talk about.

So, to blend in and appear as one of the crowd we do what the others are doing. At dinner we listen to what others are ordering. During the cocktail hour we gaze into their glass for a clue to what to drink. What is the host wearing? A tie? Ah, everything is in order, it's formal.

Put on a happy face. Look interested in the conversation of the person next to you, even if he or she is talking to someone else and you are just listening. Look as though you belong and blend in.

Everyone's watching. Careful! But is anyone really watching you at all. You're torn between wishing people would notice you and hoping they don't.

When you go to the library you want everyone to think you are very intellectual and come there all the time. Actually you are drifting up and down aisles gazing at titles in the hope that one will pop out at you and say, "Take me home with you."

Everything is done with precision and perfection while at church. We must look as though we are quite familiar with the routine. Smile, even though no one smiles back. Smile at the walls if you must, unless of course you are attending a funeral. Then you must put on your very grave expression.

In the doctor's office we wish to appear as a visitor unless we've come in on an emergency. Then we must look very, very sick so that when they call us ahead of everyone else in the room they will not glare at us because they have been there an hour.

If for any reason you find yourself in a police station, the expression to wear is, "I'm new in town and can't find the post office!"

How often when we leave our houses do we decide which personality to wear? Are we a blend or do we blend in? When we are bored stiff with a performance, a party or a meeting do we ever leave early? Do we know where we belong or do we desire to belong everywhere?

I'm not a joiner by nature. I belong to a political party, not by choice but because it is tied up with the election process. I don't feel like I belong to a political party because the one I used to be in promotes so many causes contrary to my convictions, and the one I am presently affiliated with is even more distasteful than the first.

I belong to a church where I am criticized by my liberal friends for being too conservative and by my conservative friend as being too liberal.

If anyone associates belonging with being comfortable, welcomed with open arms, or accepted for what you are—then banish such thoughts. You belong somewhere or to something because you are convinced that you belong.

Just let someone try to move you out of your place in the line at the grocery store. Not on a bet!. You'll stand your ground. Just let someone try to budge you from left to center. Not on a bet! You stand your ground. You're right even though you're left. And if you're right then you're double right.

No, we don't want a nation full of fuzzy thinkers, but perhaps a little tolerance, respect and appreciation for the people who hold views contrary to our own.

We can't all be right all of the time—and sometimes each of us take a left turn.

Needless worry about aging

On New Year's Eve we customarily place emphasis on age—the passing of one year and the coming of a new one, with the baby and "Old Father Time" as symbols. I guess it should be a reminder to most of us of where we have been and where we are going.

Just because the date on the calendar changes doesn't mean it happened in a split second. Gradually the old year has been ebbing away and we have been preparing for a new one. In our aging process one year should also gradually melt into another. We don't wake up like Rip Van Winkle some morning to find that we have aged 20 years. It happens gradually.

I believe there is much fear of aging in our country. There is constant stress on looking and feeling younger. Since youth represents a great percentage of the buying market, the fashions and music are set more to that pace. And the youth are full of new ideas and energy. Hopefully in the coming year, and years, the energy of youth and the experience of age may learn to cooperate in their efforts for achieving a better world.

In many quarters there is a resentment generated against youth in general by those who may fear aging. I'm sure that all of us elders can recall times when we felt put-down simply because of our youth. Times when our ideas were not even considered because they appeared innovative. But most of us didn't let that get us down—we just waited until we were old enough, wiser and more experienced, and then put into effect some of those same ideas that we had in our youth.

Even our outlook on life goes through a mellowing—or aging process. Among the many good thoughts that came in the Christmas mail was this one on "Growing Old Gracefully" by Author Unknown, and I will share it with you:

> "Lord Thou knowest better than I know myself that I am growing older and will one day be old.
>
> Keep me from the fatal habit of thinking I must say something on every subject and on every occasion.
>
> Release me from craving to try to straighten out everybody's affairs.
>
> Make me thoughtful but not moody, helpful but not bossy. With my vast store of wisdom, it seems a pity not to use it all—but Thou knowest, Lord, that I want a few friends at the end.
>
> Keep my mind from the recital of endless details—give me wings to get to the point.
>
> Seal my lips on my aches and pains. They are increasing and love of rehearsing them is becoming sweeter as the years go by.

Teach me the glorious lesson that occasionally I may be mistaken. Keep me reasonably sweet. I do not want to be a saint—some of them are so hard to live with—but a sour old person is one of the crowning works of the devil. Give me the ability to see good things in unexpected places and talents in unexpected people. Give me the grace to tell them so. Amen."

Fear of aging, fear of the future can be crippling. When my brother drowned and I feared the water—I learned to swim. When I had fear of appearing before people and expressing myself—I learned to act, speak and write. When I began to have twinges of fear about my fading youth I began visiting the aged in a convalescent home in California. I learned a great deal by exposure. Many of my friends would say, "I couldn't do that, I find it depressing to be around old people." The depressing part comes from a personal fear of aging.

*   *   *

I have never been able to rationalize as to why people get so smashed at a New Year's Eve party that they have to nurse a hangover during the parades and football games on New Year's Day.

I've done it more than a few times in the past—but that still doesn't answer the question of why I did it. Is this the great American custom? If it is then perhaps it is time for customs to change!

With the increasing reports on the link between drinking drivers and fatalities on the road it would appear to be the time for a massive examination of conscience. What is my obligation to my fellow man when I get behind the wheel of my car?

When you are on the road you have no idea what condition the driver of the oncoming car may be in. Defensive driving may be good to a point—but the drinking driver may outwit your best defensive efforts.

In the hands of a drinking driver the automobile can be a lethal weapon!

Concern for others is a privilege

"I'm really concerned about you!"

It was a long time since I had heard anyone say that to me. Such a long time that it touched me deeply. There are some people who have a real talent for concern for others. I am fortunate to have known many such persons.

So many of us are far away from our families of origin and we forget what it is like to have those warm, let-your-hair-down types of communication, but sometimes an acquaintance will become a friend by showing a little concern for us.

I don't think we realize fully what tremendous good we can do, and what a lift we can give another by expressing genuine concern. In this instance the person was expressing concern because I apparently looked like I had lost weight. Which in fact I hadn't.

Actions often speak louder than words but I think in this day and age we are people of words. Part of our sociability required the right word in the right place, and words, sincerely expressed are certainly actions in themselves, heard with the ear and felt with the emotions.

My mother called from Michigan (both parents now deceased) because my dad was concerned about the storm that struck in Vancouver and wondered about us. They cared.

This week, I am working on two stories about care and concern—one dealing indirectly with parents caring about their children when the children are young, and the other dealing indirectly with children caring about their parents when the parents are old.

Sometimes I feel sad when I hear about children who feel they cannot go to their parents with a problem, and they have to find another who will listen. When things like this come to my attention I try to get closer to my kids, I try to let them know that they are loved—and that I care.

It is good for kids to have other people they can go to for sharing troubles or joys, but I would hate to think it was because I had a closed ear or mind.

My kids know I'm human. They have seen me make mistakes. They see me cry. Hear me apologize when I act in haste, judge too quickly, or punish too severely. They have heard me say I'm sorry, that I love them, that I care. They have also heard me take back words that were too harsh for young ears.

Our words tell those we love many things, but sometimes we use so many words that they can't hear anything we're saying.

I'm sure I don't have to tell my readers that I think my kids are pretty special, wonderful people—and I'm sure most of you feel just the same about your young people.

And then, I talked recently to an elderly lady who has eight children who seldom visit, call or write. And I wonder, when I need love and care the most, will mine remember me? It is not pleasant to think of sitting sadly alone in your old age when those whom you cared so much for care so little in return.

It is easy to say that life goes on and everyone has to live his own life, but days are long for the elderly, with sleep the blessing that shortens the day.

Everyone needs to know someone is concerned about them—someone cares.

Holding grudges can be tiring

No matter how hard I try I can't hold a grudge—and believe me I've tried.

I admire those who can carry their grudges for months or even years. I have known such stalwarts in my life, even brothers who wouldn't speak to each other for over a year—every family has them. I've managed to carry a grudge for a week at a time, but the weight gets to be too much and I abandon the cause. Once I even carried a grudge for two weeks but found it impossible to prolong.

Perhaps something in my personality prevents me from taking this "justifiable" route of harboring secret ill will or resentment. Something in my childhood has been giving me a hang-up. I'm inhibited.

My mother came up with some strange sayings when I was growing up. When I would pout she would say "Don't go to bed mad!" or "Don't let the sun set on your anger!" The picture I got was that I might die before I woke up in the morning, and there was something about dying while angry or resentful that bothered me. It still does.

As a result of my inhibition over carrying grudges I have had to stoop pretty low on occasion. I have spoken when silence was too much. It just isn't worth the effort. Grudges are heavy beasts to carry on your shoulders.

So if you, too, want to become inhibited—make someone happy and talk to them. Maybe they won't appreciate it but you'll sure feel better.

*   *   *

My teenage son brings me recipes. He samples food at his friend's house and tells me what a wonderful cook the mother is. I could easily develop a complex about my cooking, but swallow what little pride I have left in the culinary area and tell him to ask for the recipe.

I believe it is a compliment to ask a cook for a recipe. There are very few closely guarded family secrets in the kitchen (closets yes—kitchens no).

As a compliment to the very fine German lady who translated this recipe I will pass it on to you. If you are looking for something fast, big and good for a holiday crowd try:

Mrs. Kemper's Apple Kuchen

3 and ¾ cup flour	2 eggs
½ cup sugar	2 cubes butter
2 tsp. Vanilla	or margarine

Put flour, sugar, vanilla and eggs into a large bowl and Cut margarine (butter) into it. Work like pie dough.

Roll paste ¼ inches thick and fit into cookie sheet with a rim. Top with ¼ inch apple sauce or pared and sliced apples. Sprinkle with sugar and cinnamon. Top with crumbs. (1 cup flour, 1 cup sugar, ¾ cube margarine or butter—combined). For crumbs rub between both hands until you can crumble it on top of apples. Bake at 375 degrees for 30 or 45 minutes, until crumbs are light brown or apples are soft.

Some leftover dough will be good for cutout cookies—brush with milk and sprinkle with sugar.

"New Morality"—not so new

"You're old fashioned!"

"Everyone's doing it!"

"I'm old enough to know what I'm doing!"

"Don't you trust me?"

Youthful words of rebellion have changed very little from one generation to the next. I've heard there's a "new morality" and I've tried to find out exactly what it might be. It seems rather difficult to narrow down to a commonly accepted and mutually held set of values. There are some new catch phrases that have cropped up in recent years, but they mean about the same as the old set.

"Do your own thing!"

"I'm not hurting anyone but myself—and that's my business!"

"It's all about me!"

"You can't legislate morality!"

I contend that there is no such animal as a "new morality" it's just yesterday's hash warmed over.

I went to the American Heritage Dictionary for a working definition of morality.

"Morality, 1. The quality of being moral. 2. The evaluation of or means of evaluating human conduct, as: a.) a set of ideas of right and wrong; Christian morality. b.) a set of customs of a given society, class or social group which regulates relationships and prescribe modes of behavior to enhance the group's survival. 3.

Virtuous conduct, especially in compliance with approved codes for sexual behavior."

It's difficult to find a way of fitting the concept of the "new morality" into that working definition. As I understand the promoters of the "new morality" they would have us throw off all the restrictions of the past dealing with sexual behavior and relationships.

In my book morality involves a great deal more than the sexual arena. There is a broad scope of human interrelationships involving fairness and honesty that would enter the picture. But say for an example there is a country trying to throw off all the restrictions of the past, trying to break down family ties and permanent relationship.

In November of 1917, the Bolsheviks ousted the Mensheviks from power and gained control of Russia, and the Communist movement. In December of that year a series of decrees were issued that began destroying the family and putting children under state care.

The first decree permitted marriages to be canceled by either partner without giving reason. Opposition by one party was ignored.

Incest, bigamy and adultery were taken from the list of criminal offenses. Abortion was made optional. Parents were forbidden to give religious instruction to their children. Children were encouraged to denounce their parents. Inheritance was abolished. Registered and non-registered marriages were recognized as equal.

Women began to take their meals in the communal and the state cared for their children to free them for factory work. This was required to free her from "maternal obligations so that she may produce a greater amount of work" according to Lenin.

In March of 1919, women were made the sexual possessions of the state and no longer the "private property" of one man. It was stated in the decree that "Male citizens do not have the right to use women more often than prescribed, that is, three times a week for three hours each time . . . any pregnant woman will be dispensed of her duties for four months before and three months after the birth of the child . . . One month after their birth, children will be placed in an institution . . . they will remain until age seventeen . . . . "

This movement had drastic results in the U.S.S.R., and the very existence of the country was threatened. In 1937 the population figures were 13 million behind expectations. In 1934, there were 57 thousand children born but 154 thousand abortions were performed. There were 37 divorces for every 100 marriages. By 1937 a curtailing of abortions and divorces began.

The following statement can now be read in the official journal of the Commissariat of Justice:

"The state cannot exist without the family. Marriage is a positive value for the Socialist Soviet State only if the partners see in it a lifelong union. So called free love is a bourgeois invention and has nothing in common with the principles of conduct of a Soviet citizen. Moreover, marriage receives its full value for the State only if there is progeny, and the consorts experience the highest happiness of parenthood."

I have adapted some of the research information from the book by Lucius F. Cervantes, S.J., called *"And God Made Man and Woman,"* in several of the foregoing statements.

The old saw is, "You can't legislate morality!" But it appears that you can. Enforcing the law can be another matter. Money is approved by the legislature for weaponry and war, and the president extends the draft law. The Supreme Court rules in favor of no prayer in public schools, and abortion on demand. Divorce by mutual agreement is the norm. Can it be argued that "morality" is being legislated?

There are those who tell us that times have changed and that we must change with the times. This type of "new morality" amounts to group agreement, conformity, and morality by consensus or mass hysteria. Independent thinking is frowned upon these days, especially if that thinking leans in favor of what many of us might call "clean living."

Who decides the moral order? Who decides what is right or wrong? Is there an existing pattern of order or does the group decide? Do we accept a set of values handed down for generations;

do we make our own evaluations in regard to our way of life and relationships with others; do we set our moral values based upon the approval or disapproval of our peers or superiors?

When kids hit the drug scene and they tell you that they are only harming themselves they are wrong. If you have loved ones, if you have a job, if you drive a car, you are directly or indirectly affecting the life others. Be it drugs, booze, sex or whatever, when you put ideas into action you involve others.

Before anyone accuses me of sounding like a Rush Limbaugh, let me assure you that when the above column was written and published in the newspaper in the early 1970s, I was a tad more conservative. The Cold War was on. The conflict in Vietnam divided the country, young and old. I read the column to myself and to my husband before I decided to include it in this chapter, and in this book. Today, I might pull out some of the issues and give them my current spin—but alas, that was my truth as I saw it at that time. We sometimes mellow and mature with age.

Aloofness unnatural but not uncommon

"People who need people are the happiest people in the world." This musical refrain keeps coming back and running through my brain from time to time, and each time I try to analyze it.

So often we dwell on the unhappiness and loneliness in the world and neglect to dwell on the happiness that people actually share by being together. I heard it said yesterday that poets seldom use the theme of joy—more often it is sorrow. Perhaps that is because more people can identify with sorrow than joy.

But, when you see joy in action it is contagious. So, I must share with you this experience.

As most Catholics and non-Catholics are aware, sweeping changes have occurred in the liturgical celebration of the Mass. One of the things more recently (1970s) introduced has been the "Kiss of Peace"—more often expressed by the common sign of peace, the handshake. I saw this beautifully demonstrated yesterday at the Mt. Angel Seminary.

Our oldest boy is a freshman in the junior seminary and we were there for a parent's club meeting, and the celebration of the Mass. During the "Sign of Peace" the young men reached out to one another and to their parents to share their deep feeling from within. Something generates. You have to be a dead head not to pick it up.

"Peace!" And it means so much to them that you try to put yourself in their place and experience what they do, and try to imagine what they mean by the expression. And you feel peace. And I came to the conclusion that people need people, not only for carrying one another's burdens—but also for sharing one another's joy.

Have you noticed how much peace and joy is generated by touching the hand of a little child? Letting their tiny fingers curl up inside of yours. Holding hands for lovers and expressions of friendship in handshakes; then in hours of misery holding the hand of the dying person to give strength and comfort.

How often do we want to reach out—and instead submerge that good impulse? Age teaches some us a caution that is perhaps unjustified. A child hardly ever pulls his hand away when you reach out to him in love. But as we grow older the openness changes to the gradual closing of doors. Sometimes the results are surprising when two children have been fighting and you bring them to the point of shaking hands and making up. There is something of a commitment to the other person once you have reached out to touch hands.

A commitment to love! The risk of being rejected and hurt are always present. Chances are that the times of rejection will decrease as the continued effort on the part of the one to love increases.

I must admit that shaking hands with another person means more to me now than it once did. I find myself immediately asking questions, inside myself, about the person. I think we have a common need to share something with each person we meet—really meet.

And then, one Saturday, while I was getting change for the parking meter from the clerk in a little grocery store off Burnside an old man was making his leave. He had his morning supply of wine tucked under his arm and talking, but no one was listening.

"Oh, who cares, I'm just a road bum anyway!"

What is there inside of us that holds us so aloof? There was another man in the shop besides the clerk, and they didn't even look up when the man spoke. Where was the hand reaching out in answer to that pitiful cry for help? Everything inside me cried out to reach out and say something to him—not to despair of his worth, but female reserve held me back.

How many opportunities do we miss every day to reach out to that someone who cries out for help? Far more often than our response. This troubles me. This sort of thing troubles some of our young people as well.

When I was young I had the habit of saying "good morning" to every person I passed on the street—but then so much has happened to make a woman cautious of "speaking to strangers." My mother always told me not to speak to strangers, but somehow I didn't think that meant putting my head down each time I passed someone. That's hard to do. It takes more effort to ignore someone than it does to say "Good Morning!"

In some parts of this country you can get away with greeting strangers, in other areas you can't. But every time we hold back we hurt. And eventually we build up an immunity to other people.

In a society where we have learned to hold back our emotions it may be difficult to effect a change. But it might be worth a try—why not, everything else seems to have failed.

Friendship—once in a lifetime opportunities

A true friendship is a rare and beautiful happening in our lives. My mother used to tell me if I had one true friend in my lifetime I should consider myself fortunate.

Perhaps as a result of placing friendship on such a high plane, I have at times been puzzled by the casual use of the term.

When does a person cross the line of an acquaintance into the area of friendship"

I have asked some of my children what they mean by friendship and received these answers:

"A friend is someone to do things with."

"A friend is someone to talk to and they will keep your secrets. Someone you can trust."

In searching a dictionary of quotations I found these interpretations that pleased me:

"False friends are like our shadow, keeping close to us while we walk in the sunshine, but leaving us the instant we cross into the shade."—Christian Nestell Bovee (1886-1918)

"One of the surest evidences of friendship that one can display to another is telling him gently of a fault—If any other can excel it, it is listening to such a disclosure with gratitude, and emending the error."—Edward George Bulwer (1803-1873)

"A friend that you have to buy won't be worth what you pay for him, no matter what that may be."—George D. Prentice (1802-1870)

"The difficulty is not so great to die for a friend as to find a friend worth dying for."—Henry Home (1696-1782)

"The only way to have a friend is to be one."—Ralph Waldo Emerson (1803-1882)

I like the last the best.

When the children asked what I considered the meaning of the word "friend" I said that a friend was someone I felt comfortable with. And basically I am comfortable with people I trust. People who are honestly being themselves.

Occasionally I will meet a person and like them right away because there is something so genuine about them that I say to myself, "I wish we could become friends."

The busy pace of our lives and distances (in miles) between us and the near missing caused by the circumstances of our particular way of life may prevent these acquaintances from becoming friends. But for a few moments they have enriched our lives—and it is hoped that we have enriched theirs.

Once a true friendship is established nothing can change the relationship—except perhaps the serious betrayal of a trust.

We have honored friends whom time and distance have not affected. We meet after months or years of separation and we are immediately comfortable with them again—sharing memories and experiences.

Because we have become such a mobile society, perhaps we make friends more quickly than in the past. There seems to be some urgency in getting the most out of these fleeting friendships that we can.

Do we see the potential for friendship and give the apple its name while still a blossom? And isn't that good enough for the present?

Friends and/or enemies can/can't hurt us

"Sticks and stones can break my bones but names can never hurt me!" The youthful refrain comes to mind when we think of friends and/or enemies.

A friend is someone who deliberately wants what is good for us.

An enemy is someone who deliberately wants what is not good for us.

Sometimes those who would do us harm, either physical or psychological, may turn out to be our friends in regard to the good they really force into our lives. Sometimes the good that comes from what we consider unfortunate circumstances far outweighs our fears. Frequently such circumstances put us at the crossroads of decision making.

Sometimes those who call themselves our friends can turn out to cause us more harm and less good. Often friends will unwittingly encourage us on a collision course, all the while wishing good for us. They may cause us to lean when we should stand. They may let their personal involvement in our lives distort their good judgement when giving advice. They may think they know us well, when they hardly know us at all. They may hold on to us as they would a possession without realizing the effect on them or on us.

Friends and enemies can often be interchangeable.

A mutual understanding between friends as to what they desire for the other's good may build a more solid foundation. But, a true friend may not respond as his counterpart thinks he should. For instance; one friend needs money to pay off a debt, but the other refuses to loan the money although he has plenty. The non-lender may see more good to be gained by refusing and forcing his friend to work harder or find other options to obtain the funds. The non-lender also realizes that money loaned between friends, or relatives, often separates them because one feels the burden of being in debt to the other.

If we can look at life's happenings as stepping stones rather than stumbling blocks then we can reap good results.

A person's reaction to the "sticks and stones" or even the "names" hurled at him can make or break him. In that regard he chooses to be his own best friend, or worst enemy.

Adult/child relationships built on trust

The new word among the junior high kids is NARK. I hope I'm not using a dirty word, but according to my source it means a tattle-tale. It's anybody who goes to the principal, teacher or your mom and tells something on you.

The matter of getting information to the right people has always been a problem for kids. They tell me that you should tell a friend. And a friends keeps his mouth shut.

So I posed this question. "What would you do if you had a friend standing on the window ledge of a building threatening to jump?"

"I'd try to help!" was the answer.

"What if the friend wouldn't listen to you. Would you turn your back and ignore the situation, or would you get someone to help? Maybe someone with a net," I said.

"Well, I don't know. Nothing like that has ever happened."

It is easy to have the correct answer if we are never faced with a situation.

According to the kids a friend is someone you can depend on.

"What would you do if you knew someone was on drugs and doing harm to themselves?" I asked.

"We'd tell their friends."

"What if their friends were taking drugs, too, and didn't care?"

"I don't know!" My two young friends replied.

All of the kids who don't take drugs, or don't engage in other potentially harmful activity see some of the dangers involved. But most of them don't know what to do with information about others. And so it seems that those who could do the most good in this area lack the tools.

There is always the possibility that the person will deny that they have ever "popped pills, smoked pot, shot up" or indulged in any other way. Then the person who gave out the information to be helpful ends up with egg-on-face, and becomes a social outcast.

There have been a few different versions of attempting to get information from those in the know. Our local high school administration once sent out forms with stamped, self-addressed envelopes to encourage kids to anonymously supply information. Another school district group is attempting an anonymous phone call system to crack down.

If you ask parents what their biggest concern is they will usually tell you it's the drug problem.

Hopefully our society will come up with the right answers soon. If friends are those people you can trust, those people you can depend on, then we had better look into improving the situation by establishing the kind of rapport that makes a kid aware of friendship. Not a friendship in relationship to age, but one that will cross barriers.

Following this same train of thought, the kids tell me that the other big word around school is HYPOCRITE.

"A hypocrite is like someone who tells you that smoking is dangerous to your health and holds a lighted cigarette in the hand he's pointing with," I said in response to their questions about the meaning of the word.

In trying to follow their line of reasoning I would guess that they wouldn't choose a "hypocrite" for a friend because they think that being a "hypocrite" is a pretty bad scene.

I guess all of us from time to time have to ask ourselves, "Am I really real?" Everything is so new, moving so fast, and subject to change that it is difficult to maintain a steady course along our chosen path. Without engaging in excessive self-criticism, it is good for kids to know that age does not bring perfection, but hopefully wisdom.

Age may bring about knowledge of right, but it is still as hard to practice what we preach as it ever was.

*   *   *

The new Sears' "Wish Book" is out and everyone around here is getting that holiday itch. The children are already pointing out what they would like for Christmas.

Right on the heels of "What kind of candy are you getting for Halloween" they ask, "Who are you inviting for Thanksgiving?" and tell you "I want . . . for Christmas."

I keep telling them that they have it all wrong with the gimmes; there is no Santa. There is a Mommy and a Daddy who decide how much to spend and on what.

From now on we will be bombarded with TV commercials telling the little ones to "ask your mommy and daddy about this one, kids!" You have to start early to keep the kids pointed away from the materialism of the holiday season. It would be a shame if when they grow up the only thing they remember about Christmas is what presents they got.

*   *   *

On the way home from church this morning one of the kids gave me this choice bit of information. The word "nincompoop" is in the dictionary. I'll bet you didn't know that. It's defined as a "fool, simpleton or blockhead." The dictionary also says, "origin unknown." Which means that somewhere out there in this great world of ours some bright person made up the word and the rest of us picked it up and used it enough to gain it recognition in the American Heritage Dictionary.

So, if you have an urge to be known for something great, you too can make up a word that will live on long after you are gone.

Wedding in the family

Months of preparation culminated in the wedding day for our oldest daughter. Then in a flurry and a flash the ceremony and reception were all over. The bride and groom left for their honeymoon and then I felt what most parents feel—a tremendous set of mixed emotions.

Happiness for the new couple.

Realization that a child had grown up and would forever more return home as an adult.

A slight emptiness that I couldn't attempt to explain.

A sense of relief that one offspring was self-sufficient.

Regrets that some of the day's events couldn't have been more pleasant, brighter, happier, totally untainted.

A sinking feeling thinking of the potential five more times that we would be the parents of the bride.

Sorrow because the emotion that welled up in me couldn't find words of expression or an avenue for sharing.

Years later I would look back at the wedding pictures and compare that day's event with my own wedding day and remember that I was in nearly as much of a daze during one as during the other.

The night my granddaughter was born

We were watching a movie on television about a pregnant woman whose lover had apparently been some occupant of a ship from outer-space.

"I hope Diane isn't watching this," one of the children said as she chewed her fingernails.

Then the phone rang. Our oldest daughter was in labor and heading for the hospital. My husband was packed and heading for his 25-year class reunion in Michigan in the morning. I changed clothes and started the 110-mile drive to the hospital.

I knew the baby would be born whether or not I was there. But I felt compelled to be there and will forever be grateful that I could.

I got to the hospital in record time, but my daughter was already in the delivery room. For the first time I found out what it was like to spend time in the waiting room—waiting for a baby to be born. I had gone through eight labors and deliveries and didn't know how to act on the outside of it all.

My daughter and her husband had attended childbirth classes together because they wanted the birth of their child to be a shared experience. My son-in-law was with her throughout labor and delivery. (A wonderful new concept from when I had my babies.)

Then he came into the waiting room to tell me the news of a baby girl. He took me to the recovery room where Diane held her newborn in her arms. My son-in-law took the infant from its mother and placed her in my arms. I looked at the baby and her parents, and for one of the rare moments in my life I was speechless.

"Thank God," was all I could think and say. Thank God my daughter was doing well after delivery. Thank God a child was born who might not have been. In the very early days of pregnancy my daughter had gone to a doctor for a back problem and he took multiple X-rays. Later, when the obstetrician found out about it he said there might be a problem with the baby and left the couple the option of abortion. They agonized over the decision for a week, contacting many authorities in the field—and the result of their decision rested peacefully in my arms, minutes old and perfectly beautiful.

No more fear of success

Only I knew the blood, sweat and tears that went into the reception of my bachelor's degree. College study began 24 years prior, before my marriage. I gradually acquired additional credits until I determinedly faced the issue and drove full speed ahead to reach my goal.

When there are more than 1,000 students who expect to receive degrees many of them decide in advance not to attend the graduation ceremony. I decided to be measured for cap and gown and go through the ritual. It meant that much to me. And apparently to my family, for they all decided to attend—even my granddaughter in her stroller.

When the honor students assembled before the graduation ceremony we discovered we would be sitting on the stage of the Civic Auditorium during the program. It gave me a perfect view of my family. I spotted them on my way in and had a better view of them than they did of me.

And when they asked me what I would do with my degree I smiled proudly, knowing my hard work had earned me entrance into graduate school and a fellowship, the opportunity for concentrated study in communications and classroom experience as a teaching assistant.

Certainly it was worth the effort.

Skeletons in the closet

Every family has them. Every writer makes information choices and I believe in the family's and the individual's right to privacy.

Personal tragedy and sorrow find other modes of expression— if the writer truly has something worthwhile to say on a subject.

There are moments of deep depression, feelings of being totally inadequate to meet the demands of the circumstances of our lives. We are frustrated with conflicting needs and goals, and harbor deep sorrow for the harm we have done to others—and the hurt we ourselves feel as the result of the actions of others.

Roll with the punches, bounce back, recover, and continue— we have to, because the survival instinct is so much a part of our humanity. It's not such a bad idea to keep those skeletons locked away—so we know where they are.

Happy New Year!—every day

What does a New Year hold for us? I leave predictions to others and just hope for the best.

It's time to renew old resolutions that proved too much for us in years past. It's time to close the ledger on the passing year's monetary considerations and transactions in preparation for the income tax return. When you add it all up you wonder where it all went.

I don't usually make resolutions a year ahead because I'm not that far sighted and too many things are subject to change. I don't smoke, drink, or need to lose weight. (The weight thing has changed.) So it boils down to the resolutions that we make to ourselves every day. Try to keep my house in order as best I can.

There are books gathering dust on the shelf that belong to someone else. Each year, near the end, I go over the shelves and pull the borrowed items for return, even if I haven't had time to read them. It's time to return them with a note of thanks. Many times people have forgotten about the particular book and its whereabouts, and they are surprised and pleased at the reminder. Usually they tell you to go ahead and keep it longer—but then maybe they need or want it themselves.

I know people who never loan books, they give them away. That relieves them of wondering where it is and when it will be returned. I have acquired several books from people who feel it's useless to loan them. Some of the books that people "give" to me get returned anyway, because I know they will enjoy "giving them away" again.

The books we receive as gifts remind us of friends, and carry some of their personality across the years or miles to us just as a photograph might do.

In organizing my book shelves at the close of the year I also clean my files. If I'm hurried I dump everything drifting about the desk into a large box to be filed at leisure.

The list of things that I didn't get done last year is still too long to bother about making a new list.

So, Happy New Year—one day at a time.

VII

PEOPLE I CAN'T FORGET

The human personality is like a prism dangling from a string in the window and reflecting the dancing, changing color patterns of sunlight on the table tops of our impressions.

As a writer/interviewer/reporter it has been my privilege to probe my own personality and the personality of many others—hundreds, in fact. Most people don't realize the amount of sifting, sorting and agonizing choices that go into a story based on an interview. There are so many ways to present a personality, and we writers always hope we have stayed as close to the facts as humanly possible. As we perceive life, so we report it.

The good people we never read about

Some of the best stories will never be written. As I mentally go through a decade of interviews and photographs, I recall many incidents where I've had to leave out interesting items or drop a story completely.

Most of the information will eventually find expression in fact or fiction, or give rise to other ideas that can be developed.

I have great respect for the printed word and it should be handled with care. The rights of others to be secure in their privacy and preference for anonymity must be respected.

Most people like to have their picture taken for publication. Even though some voice objections, you know it's modesty holding them back. There's some embarrassment in facing a camera and some difficulty setting the subject at ease. I usually keep talking all the time I'm taking pictures, and get my subject to talk back to me.

Often a camera appears as an intruder on the scene. I suppose most of us are getting used to seeing flashes of light during the solemn moments of a wedding or during religious services. It takes a particular type of person to get the job done, to leave a permanent record of an event without antagonizing spectators and participants.

A photographer can't be timid. Fast action is vital, as a rule. There isn't always time for diplomacy. I'm basically rather timid. Many times I've had to overcome that timidity rather than leave without a photo. Photography is probably the most challenging part of my recording of events and people.

When I haven't done news features or interviews for a time I have to overcome the initial reluctance to probe, explore and question my interview subject. Every person has an interesting story to tell and it's my job to pull it out of them and report it as best I can.

Not everyone wants the world to know the good they do. Sometimes the person goes the limit and refuses to be interviewed or photographed. Most people can be convinced that their story should be in print when appealed to on the basis of helping others.

Unfortunately, the day-to-day goodness of people isn't always newsworthy. When I was doing weekly feature stories for the community paper I made an effort to dig up good stories about ordinary people. Sometimes the ones with the most to say and the most to offer are also the most reluctant to be interviewed and receive recognition in publication.

There are, indeed, more good people in this world than any of us realize—or ever read about.

Mailmen I have known

A visitor comes to our house nearly every day of the year. He or she is often unnoticed and seldom acknowledged.

If he were still thundering up the dusty road on his trusty

steed we would dry our hands of soapsuds at the kitchen sink and run out to the front of the house at the first sound of approaching hoof-beats. Instead, we simply lift the lid of the mailbox and scoop out the messages, bills and advertising.

On holidays I systematically make my trip to the mailbox— then remember he won't be there today. There's a momentary sinking feeling somewhere inside as I feel cut off from the outside world.

When I was a child he brought birthday greetings from relatives far away. I waited for him each day as the birthday drew near. And when an envelope bore my name I'd rip it open and shake the card to see if a coin or a bill would fall out, then I would read the message on the card and find out who sent it.

A pen pal in a distant city had me looking eagerly through the daily mail when I returned from school. Much happiness came with each grand opening, though the scrawled script may have merely stated, "Hi, I'm fine. How are you? Our cat had three kittens. It's getting cold out. Write soon."

Then came the love letters. A young women in love cherishes the tender messages from the object of her affections when they're too many miles apart for the luxury of phone calls. Sometimes I waited on the front steps as the mailman slowly made his way from house to house. I tried to hide my impatience but he detected my anxiety and quickened his pace when he neared the house. The letter from an Air Force sergeant in New Mexico was always on top, and if a day was missed my mailman supported me with a sad smile.

Mailmen around the country carried happy news of a wedding announcement, and later they delivered the word as each baby made an appearance. Mailmen are still carrying an occasional letter to friends and relatives around the country, but since I started writing professionally I've become stingy with my correspondence— a sad commentary indeed. (Thank God for modern technology and E-mail.)

I'm still delighted with the fact that through the mail a part of me can go where most of me cannot.

Sorting through a pile of unwanted mail may often bring an exciting piece of information. Among the bids to buy our clothes mail-order we may find a bargain for the collected works of Shakespeare bound in imitation red leather. Perhaps we discover a letter from a friend hidden among the advertising, and our faith in humanity is restored as we're reminded that someone out there cares.

A great deal of my writing business is conducted via the US Postal Service (and now, E-mail). Manuscripts for articles or short stories go out, and when the large manila envelope shows up on a return trip to my mailbox I repair my ego and send it out again. Communications and sales to magazine editors have built up over the years and my mailman brings me more good news and rewards than I ever expected.

Thanks, Mr. Mailman or Ms. Mailman. I've never really known you, and have often taken you for granted—but I do appreciate all you've done for me.

The Archbishop smiled and the camera jammed

My first adventure into journalism came as a result of answering an ad in the local paper. They wanted a correspondent who was interested in learning how to use a camera.

I boasted that I had my first photo published on the front page of our suburban daily in Michigan when I was a mere 15. Then, when the supplement came out at the end of that year, touting the best pictures of the year, my photo was on the front page and tag-lined as the only picture taken by an amateur to be so honored in the section.

My claim-to-fame photo came from a simple box camera. We lived near the railroad tracks, and a huge chemical plant blocked our view of the trains. Several times each year the chemical pots boiled over and smoke and fire flew up the stacks. The fire engines came and crowds gathered to watch. Usually this phenomenon occurred in the dark of night. Once it happened in broad daylight.

We had just returned from vacation and my father prompted

me to take my loaded camera outside and shoot. By the time the newspaper photographer appeared on the scene everything had died down. My father told him about my roll of film and the photographer took it in for developing and printing. I received $5, a set of 8x10 black and white glossy prints, and recognition.

Many years after the fire, I was performing correspondent duties for the local paper. I was ready to establish myself as a reporter-photographer. I summed up my courage and asked for an assignment to interview the retired Catholic Archbishop of the Portland Archdiocese.

One of the results of my 11 years in the Catholic school system was that I still held the clergy in awe. And an Archbishop represented considerable authority. Frankly, I was scared.

Archbishop Edward D. Howard was 90 years young at the time I interviewed him. He will occupy a special place in my memory for his gracious manner. He welcomed me into his home and allowed me to select a chair in the good light of the wide bay window. I set up my tape recorder with his approval and then tried to relax with poised pen and open notebook.

We discussed his family and my family. His schooling and my schooling. Then I eased into the controversial issue of birth control—that's what my editor wanted me there for in the first place. The Archbishop took his position with that of the Pope's, and I faithfully recorded his quotes.

When the interview wound up, as the recording tape ran out, I asked if he would please pose for a picture. He stood before the ornate fireplace between two large imported alabaster vases and smiled as he looked at the aged photographs of his deceased parents. And the camera I'd taken with me from the newspaper office jammed.

I made a feeble attempt to cover up my unfamiliarity with the camera I'd been given and begged his indulgence while I left to get another camera. I returned in half an hour and shot the pictures I needed. He knew my embarrassment and cooperated with all the kindness implied in his title, "Your Grace."

John White at age 102

The first time I interviewed John white he was 102 years old. It matters little how many years he lived beyond that time, for it is my purpose to present him frozen in time as I would with a photograph. That way he can live on, and on.

I was working on a story at the junior high school when one of the teachers told me about an elderly gentleman of 102 who had visited a social studies class and talked about his early years. The teacher remarked on how well the man related to the young people and how clear his mind seemed to be.

An excited idea presentation to my editor brought questions about a hook or angle for the story. It seemed to me that being 102 was angle enough for any story, and his personality would have to dictate the treatment. So, I made the contacts and set up the interview.

John White lived in a comfortable suburban house at the end of a road in a heavily wooded area. His son and daughter-in-law both worked, so he busied himself during the day by washing the dishes, taking care of his room, watering the lawn and flowers, taking long walks to the store, watching TV, and playing several games of Solitaire. And if you watched him closely you would discover why he was often a winner.

Hefty ankle-high walking shoes, suit pants, long-sleeve white shirt and tie, with a cable-knit bright blue vest neatly clothed a slim figure of a man. He boasted of his 53 years and six months with the Jones Lumber Company, where he could do anything and everything in the place. He retired at age 80, with much reluctance, when his son insisted he had worked long enough.

I don't know what I expected to see or hear when I arranged the interview, certainly not the bright, twinkling-eyed, soft-spoken ex-lumberman who sucked on mint candies while expressing his preference for chewing tobacco. A man with thinning white hair, no excess flesh on his face, who enjoyed a good pair of eye glasses, cuddled a dog named "Magoo" and a cat named "Cat," and honored his guest with sweet melodic singing.

John White liked to pluck the strings on the banjo and forgot a few words when he sang "Sam Johnson was a Marching Man" and "Casey Jones."

The tape recorder kept turning and I took few notes as I gradually fell under the spell of the enchanting little man nestled into a comfortable chair, spinning yards of yarn from his past. Sometimes his daughter-in-law interrupted to help him put the story in proper chronological order and remind him of an interesting event. I suppose when you've got more than 100 years of remembering to do you might even get a wife, a son or a war out of proper sequence.

John White was born in Pison "not poison" Cove, Tennessee. He spent most of his youth driving mule trains. When he was 10 he drove a 10-head mule train, "of course, I rode one of them," he said. "We made a round trip once a week. A man followed the train, when a wheel broke he fixed it and we kept going."

When it was time for school there just weren't any schools, so he skipped the educational process of the classroom and gathered his experiences on the outside.

When his friends enlisted in the Spanish-American War he "went along with the bunch" and changed his name to "Black" for no particular reason, just for the fun of it, to be someone else. A time later he did a singing and dancing vaudeville tour down the West Coast from Seattle to San Francisco.

John White loved parades. He'd stood for hours watching the Portland Rose Festival Parade the year before.

"Have you ever been in a parade?" An idea was coming to me.

"No, never have." I observed a wistful smile.

"Would you like to ride in a parade?" I was thinking about the Beaverton Diamond Jubilee Parade about two weeks in the future, and knew this man had to be a participant.

Later that day I made a few short phone calls. The Hollywood star Grand Marshal for the parade had canceled and John White was going to be contacted to be the Grand Marshal—riding at the head of the parade in a classic touring car with the top down. Then he would sit on the reviewing stand and watch the rest of the parade go by.

A large banner on the sides of the car proclaimed the name and age of John White, a truly distinguished senior citizen, and he smiled and waved as he received the cheers and applause of the crowd.

Forgotten wars and remembered people

News cools quickly. Wars are fought, forgotten, and filed away with annual reports to stockholders and scuttled revenue sharing plans.

But the people. The people who live through the wars, fight the wars, feel the pains of war—should not be forgotten, and sometimes cannot be forgotten.

It was more than a routine interview for the newspaper. An interview that motivated the hovering dove to swoop right down and demolish the hesitant hawk.

She roasted under the hair dryer in the local beauty salon, the news reporter with the sensitive nose for feature stories. The heat of an Oregon summer matched the temperature of the hot air blowing from the hair dryer late in 1970, when the Vietnam War generated its own kind of heat among young and old around the country.

The newswoman plotted and planned her story coverage for the coming week. She mentally compiled a list of Saturday chores yet to be assigned and accomplished at home, and tried to figure a way of getting a story that plagued her for weeks. How to bring the Vietnam War issue home to the suburban weekly readers? How to make the news meaningful and palatable? She wanted a perspective as fresh as a recently returned veteran—home from the war, but, not just any veteran.

The bell on the hair dryer rang. Hot air stopped blowing. The reporter lifted the hood away from her head and waited for the beautician to finish trimming the long blond hair of a high school girl in blue jeans and T-shirt.

"Hear anything from your brother?" the beautician asked as she ran her comb down the full length of the girl's hair.

"He's coming home," the effervescent teenager with sparkling blue eyes smiles at her own reflection in the mirror.

"Great! He's been in hospital work, hasn't he?"

"Yeah, he'll sure be glad to get out of Vietnam."

The reporter reached for her purse, took out a business card and freed herself from the grasp of the hair dryer at the same time the girl readied herself to leave after paying the beautician. The two met near the door.

"Excuse me, I'm a reporter for the Community Press. I overheard what you were saying about your brother and I would love to interview him when he comes home. I want some fresh impressions of Vietnam."

"Gee, I don't know. I don't know if he'll want to."

"Just give me your phone number and I'll call him. I'll leave my card with you and you can let me know when he'll be in." Gaining cooperation for interviews seldom presented a problem, the reporter was reassured when the girl reluctantly, but finally, wrote her brother's name and phone number on a slip of paper.

"He won't be home for another two weeks," she relaxed her face with a smile and reached for the door handle.

Three weeks later an exchange of phone calls verified a morning hour for the interview.

"Do you mind if I use a tape recorder? The reporter checked.

"It'd be okay, I guess. How do you know I'll say anything worth writing about?" A slight nervous hesitancy projected over the phone.

"I don't know for sure, but I have strong feelings you'll do just fine." The reporter breathed sighs of relief after convincing Tom James he'd be performing a public service by expressing his views for the readers in suburbia, overcoming his apprehension regarding recognition and over exposure.

Tall trees lined the curbed and side-walked suburban street of homes three blocks from the high school, bus stop and gas station. Petunias clustered in colorful combinations outside the front door of the James house and it was still early enough in the day for the full-breasted robins to be singing and chattering. Tom opened the door in response to the bell.

"Hi, let me help you with the tape recorder," a clear-complexioned young man with well trimmed sandy-red hair and a soft smile extended his hand for the recorder held by the reporter.

"Thank you, just tell me where you'd like to sit and I'll tell you where we can put the recorder." Tom motioned to the sofa and nestled into one corner of the sprawling and comfortably furnished living room.

"Let's start with some of your background," the reporter settled into a well cushioned chair and trained her attention on the man across the room sitting on the edge of a sofa cushion, appearing calm but not quite all at home.

"I graduated from high school in 1965. Then I spent about a year down in Australia."

"What'd you do down there?" The reporter made her note pad inconspicuous and Tom quickly forgot about the tape recorder.

"I went down with two friends of mine. We surfed, worked, and traveled all around."

"Was that part of any project?'

"Just our own personal project," he smiled and relaxed more. "We wanted to take time out to see what was going on somewhere else. But," the tone of his voice faded for a moment and he pulled himself back to the present, "that's a whole different subject. I love the people down there and everything else. They're just great. I'm going to return. But, I'm going to get a degree first."

"A degree in what?"

"Probably just General Studies. I love biology, but now, I want to know a little bit about everything." Tom still leaned forward with his hands clasped and extended across his knees. He wore a pastel, stripped shirt with long sleeves and an unbuttoned, button-down collar, and white Levis and a wide stripe fabric belt.

"Do you think that's the way a lot of boys are when they come back? They have a whole new outlook?" And the reporter cringed at her use of the word "boys."

"Yeah!" Tom laughed, and it was a good sound. "It does change you a little bit. In the Army you're forced to be with people you wouldn't naturally associate with. And, it's good because you meet a lot of people that come from different walks of life. They usually turn out pretty interesting. And the friends you make, under the circumstances, you know, over there, are good friends.

"In other words, when you're both hiding under a bunker or something, peeking out and watching the flares and listening to the mortars, then, ugh, it's a real strong bond—because it's something you share, and, something you wouldn't share back here in the United States."

The tape recorder continued its steady pace in relative silence. Passing cars and children playing across the street delivered subdued sounds into the room where childhood and school years of happy, ghostly memories hid themselves within the walls. Tom James teetered between two worlds, the world of war in Vietnam and the world he left and was trying to re-enter. Behind his glossed-over, far-away look a collage of memories begged release.

The man who'd cheered his football, basketball and baseball teams on to victory, and thrilled at the sight of microscopic particles in the biology lab, reflected on where he was two years ago when he received his draft notice.

He loved the sciences and worked as a teacher's assistant for a couple of years in high school biology. When he went into the army he asked them if there was anything like biology he could do.

"I mean, like I was pretty naïve when I came in. I didn't even know you could enlist. I just thought they either caught you or they didn't. Now I'm glad, cause I wouldn't have enlisted anyway. According to test scores they tell you what you can qualify for in the Army.

"They said I could be an MP, or a Medic, or go to OCS and become a Second Lieutenant. But you had to extend for a year, so I told them 'Well, I'll try a Medic just to see what it's like."

So, Tom James went to Texas for 10 weeks of basic medical training. And from there went up to advanced-training in operating room technician school. He said that it was interesting and would never have had that chance to learn about surgery if he hadn't been in the field.

"But then again," Tom pondered, "I don't especially want to go back. I don't ever want to work in another hospital. I had plenty. I mean, they bring in wounded people 24 hours a day, all night and all day. And you work about 12 hours, and if you worried about each guy that goes through there you'd go nuts. Because you'd just become worthless. And if you don't worry about 'em it seems you're not doing the best job you could. I just get callous. I do the best job I can but you can't worry about everybody. You just do your job and that's it. You just become a mechanical extension of the surgeon's arm. He wants this, hold this, or cut this little tie, and you do it."

Tom spent five months duty in the hospital in Can Tho on the Mekong River in Vietnam. "Hospitals are temporary things," he said. "We work on a man as soon as he comes from the field. He has all his clothes on, boots on, his weapon still clutched in his hand, flown in by helicopter in fifteen minutes.

"We get a lot of injured at the same time. We have a doctor who looks right down the line and has to make a snap judgment— which are so badly shot up they probably won't make it. They set them aside in what is called the 'expectant file,' expected to die. It seems cold, but they're usually 99 percent right."

In the hospital facility that Tom describes as beautiful there are 20 doctors working around the clock shifts, a pathologist, chemist and a doctor for prescriptions always on duty.

"Who takes care of the Vietnamese?" The reporter had nearly lost control of the interview and wrapped herself into the feelings of the young man who seemed intent on telling his story once he began.

"Our regular doctors. And I'll tell you something that's strange. You get a V.C. casualty in and let's say it's a craniotomy, you know, he's been shot in the head. You've got to tie up all those instruments on maybe a two or three hour case, maybe two surgeons, two technicians like myself and a nurse. And what if you bring in three or four more Americans who are wounded in the same way. Ugh, it makes you wonder if a doctor's promise that he's always going to help everybody to the best of his ability and everything—if it's right in that situation."

"I guess a doctor has to be somewhat impartial," the reporter asked.

"Well, yeah, in there. Like some Viet Cong are probably mistreated in prisoner of war camps and everything else. But, in surgery they all get the same care. Everybody. It doesn't matter who they are."

"That may be the one who can be an informer?"

"Right, so you may actually be saving a lot of lives."

"Does this happen often? Are they interrogated?"

"Yeah. They (the military) interrogate them quite a bit. I've heard they have quite a few practices. They may fly. They may catch two of the Viet Cong and fly them up about a thousand feet, threaten to throw one of them out, and the other starts talking real quick. I don't know if you should print that.

"And they (the military) take away your pictures. Like when I came back. I'm searched thoroughly to make sure I don't bring narcotics and guns and everything back into the United States. One of the things they go through is your pictures. If you have pictures of government installations and things like that they take 'em and throw 'em in a big box, you know, and you're never going to see those again, because possibly it would give the enemy an insight into our organization.

"More likely it'd help the GI coming home to explain a little better what's going on over there to his family and friends. Like a lot of equipment I think is just being wasted, rusting away, or they sell it to the Vietnamese—or they give it to them and they sell it back to us. And they take away those pictures. I had a few of surgery. A friend took pictures of me working in surgery and I mailed those home, and apparently they weren't checked or anything else."

"What was your rank?"

"I remained a Pfc. For the 17 months because I do my job but

I don't believe in shining boots and clipping my hair so the skin shows on both sides of my head. I have a perfectly clean record as far as the Army goes, but I was probably considered unpromotable because I helped publish a paper over there in which we commented sarcastically about the organization. Maybe it did them a little good, and it did us a little good. It was like, we got things off our chest."

"What was the name of the paper?"

"We called it *The Fungus*. Cause over there everything seems to turn to green fungus."

"Do you think we're justified in being in Vietnam?"

"With so many people wondering, especially my generation, with all these riots, campus revolutions, and peace marches—apparently not all of the United States is in favor of our involvement in Vietnam. If they're not, then I hate to think of all the guys over there that got shot, or even those who spent a whole year over there.

"A lot of guys may be wounded mentally. When I came back the first siren I heard I hit the floor. I don't do it anymore. And I wasn't over there that long. I wasn't in the infantry. But, everybody pulls guard unless they're conscientious objector. I'd hate to think all those guys got hurt for no reason. If they said let's all get out of Vietnam, that's just admitting we had no business there in the first place.

"So, in that sense, they can't say 'let's de-escalate the war and let's all leave.' If they say that they admit they were wrong. But, at the same time, I don't like to see anybody getting hurt, no matter what the reason.

"My perspective is one of a Pfc. In what I understand of the world situation, I'd just like to stay home. But after being there a while you do feel sorry for the people. They have a real low standard of living. They can't help but have it because everything's disrupted. As far as I can tell it'll be a hundred years before they're worth anything anyway."

"You mean, before the people can bring themselves up to a productive level?"

"Yeah. Ah, I think communism will probably bring them up to a productive level quicker than we will. Because right now the people make their living off the service. Any country where there's a war the main industry surrounds the army post, or navy base. Ladies come in and clean your boots and clean your clothes and get maybe two or three dollars a month from each GI, and maybe work for ten of them.

"The black market's just huge. They sell sheets and beer and stuff like that, and it all goes to the whore houses. And they seem to make more money than the hard-working farmer. They can't afford a motor cycle and nice clothes, and the guy who used to be the mainstay of the economy, you know, he tilled his land, and the little shop keeper—nobody wants what he's got anymore. So it's disrupted their whole economy."

"Where is their food coming from now?"

"I imagine we give them a lot of food. And the food they have is a, well, they like it. It's got quite an order to it."

"What do they eat?"

"Rice, that's the main thing. And fish. They make a fish sauce that's pretty potent. I think they ferment it a little. But they sprinkle that on just about everything and it makes it good—as far as they are concerned."

Tom James couldn't seem to grasp the thought of rioting in the streets of America. "It's hard to picture that people are getting killed back here. It's real strange. A friend of mine was killed in an automobile accident and it was hard for me to believe. With the riots the guys were wondering what they were going home to.

"Everybody's picture of home becomes one-sided. It's the best place in the world. Utopia. Everybody thinks—good food, going to the refrigerator and picking out what you like, sleeping in on Saturday morning. All that seems like a real dream. Then you get news that 2,000 Hippies in San Francisco fought with the police for two hours. It really turned you off. Over there you like to think everything will be the exact opposite when you get back."

He finally relaxed back into the upholstery of the sofa and

continued his gaze out the large picture window into the greenery of the back yard rather than speak directly to the reporter.

"I'd love for people to write more letters. It does bring you back to the real world. That's what they call it over there. The United States is the 'real world.' It brings you back for just five minutes. You're back home. Back on the block and it's great. It doesn't last very long but you can read it again and just about get back a second time. And for the guys who didn't get back. I really hope this whole thing is worthwhile. That they died for a real good reason. Because if they didn't, then there should be some men in higher parts of our government that should have a very troubled conscience.

A completed interview. Rewind the tape. Pack up the notebook. Take a posed candid picture with the 35mm camera. Get rid of the lump in the throat. Shake the cobwebs out of the "justifiable war" thinking. Climb back into the Chevrolet station wagon and think like hell about the experience of one hour's worth of interview, the spilling out of guts and truth and perspective, and bringing the reality of war closer to home.

Can a reporter transfer, with integrity, the feelings of her subject? Can she get across to the reader the impact that this young man has had on her life?

Where did the hawk go? I've always favored doves anyway. Why does war have to be? Why in the hell can't we prevent it from happening again? Don't we learn anything from past experiences? Why can't the rest of the world want peace as much as we think we do?

Tom James' words go through my head on the way home.

"I didn't like gray weather. To me it seems to be a reflection when the weather is dull and gray. I spent a lot of time in the sunshine, but since I've come back from Vietnam it looks much better. It's clean, and green and quiet. That's what I noticed most. It's quiet. In Vietnam, every night, I don't care what part of Vietnam you're in, you hear the noises of war. You hear outgoing artillery and incoming mortar rounds, and you hear the helicopters all the time. They just seem to cover all of Vietnam all the time like a hive of bumble bees."

I stared at the flashing red, left-turn signal on the car in front of mine, waiting for the traffic signal to turn green—the perfect order of our civilization.

Christmas trees, traffic lights, snowball fights, supermarkets, go-carts, track meets, cheerleaders, report cards, year books, homecoming dances, kisses under the mistletoe and Fourth of July fireworks—a culture away from war, where dreams grow strong and fade away all in the same day.

Ice cream cones, Baby Ruth bars, apple pie, potato chips, Americana hamburgers deluxe with cheese, telephones and drive-in movies, friends coming to the house, laughing over crazy jokes, and Cokes—while mortar shells break sleep and blood oozing from deep open wounds. War in living color in living rooms, and quickly turned off and forgotten. One election quickly follows another. One politician promises to end war, another promises to keep the peace, and another promises to make the world safe for Democracy.

Americans lick their wounds and go back to the Sunday funnies. When the sounds of war rumble again in the land they'll wake with a startled bounce, polarize their views and begin to remember all they had hoped to forget.

I went home. Listened to the tape-recorded interview. Wrote the story. And cried.

Children—victims of war

I promised my children we'd invite Nguyen Trung, 14, and Nguyen Van Phuong, 11, to our house for dinner. The two South Vietnamese war victims were in the United States for medical and surgical treatment, and I fell in love with them months earlier when I did a story for the newspaper.

Both boys came from villages outside Saigon. One was injured when run over by an Army truck, and the other was severely burned when he walked across a open mine field—and went through a series of 60 skin grafts. The older boy had developed a bone infection and would have lost his leg had he not been brought to the United States for surgery.

The boys were brought to the U.S. by the Committee for Responsibility, a group of physicians formed for the purpose of treating war injured and war burned youth.

When I brought the boys to the house a few days before Halloween they already had months of treatment on their legs. And, although they still limped they had made remarkable improvement. The language barrier between the children proved to be insignificant, and the boys were delighted to ride the bikes. Phuong, 11, being rather small for his age was quite satisfied with a tricycle.

They played football in the street, 4-square in the driveway, worked jigsaw puzzles and carved pumpkins. Trung, 14, carved a jack-o-lantern with a sharp knife and artistry. He carved only the orange exterior, exposing the white of the pumpkin. And of course, the eyes were slanted. Other features were markedly oriental rather than the traditional western Halloween artwork. When he finished the last careful, delicate touches he handed the pumpkin to my oldest son with a broad smile—a bond of friendship.

The two boys from Vietnam played with our new puppies and were fascinated with our push-button light switches. For lunch I gave them hot dogs and Franco-American Spaghetti, and wondered if they were polite or reluctant when they waited for everyone else to start eating. Half way through the hot dog the oldest boy said "very good." They refused cookies in favor of apples. They hadn't picked up the American love of sweets. After a turkey dinner that evening they again preferred apples to sweets.

We wanted to have them come back again but knew they'd be leaving soon for their own country. We knew they'd be safer here than in Vietnam, but that was home and the place where they had family waiting. The boys didn't know each other in Vietnam. They looked like brothers to us, and treated each other with the greatest kindness.

As far as I know Phuong and Trung returned to their homes in 1969. Much later, Saigon fell to the Communists. And, as each

Halloween approaches I'm still reminded of the beautifully carved pumpkins and smiles of friendship.

If they're still alive, Nguyen Trung would be 21 and Nguyen Van Phuong, 18 (as of 1986). Hopefully they have grown into manhood just as my oldest son has.

Learning gratitude from a skid road bum

Every major city has its skid road area and its bums, its do-gooders, and its good-doers. I don't have a heart of gold. I have a heart of mush, and have to work very hard at not being a soft touch.

I read a small item in the church paper about the Blanchet House of Hospitality needing additional turkeys and other food stuffs for the Thanksgiving Day dinner to feed the dropouts and outcasts of society living on skid road in Portland. I packed the kids in the car and went out and bought the biggest turkey I could find. Not because of a sudden burst of benevolence, but rather to soothe a nagging conscience. This is why.

I'd been shopping, it was lunch-time, and I was hungry. I drove into the parking lot of a Denny's restaurant. An old man in a long gray overcoat was slouching along the sidewalk picking up cigarette butts and asking passers-by for a handout. A worn cloth hat practically hid a lined and tired, bearded face. I ignored him as I headed toward the restaurant door. The hostess seated me by the window, where I ate lunch and watched the old man rubbing his hands to keep warm on a day that smacked of winter approaching. I wanted to help, but suppressed that urge to do something good. I wanted to bring him in and watch him eat a bowl of hot soup across the table from me. He hadn't asked me for help. I was eating— and he wasn't—and it hurt.

So, when I took the turkey to Blanchet House I asked if there was anything else I could do. The director told me that I could come down and help serve meals if I wanted, so I did.

I put a turkey in the oven for our family dinner early Thanksgiving morning and dropped the kids off at a Disney movie around noon. Then I headed for skid road—a little uneasy.

There were men lined up all the way around the block, and a couple of women near the door at the head of the line. I tried not to stare, but could feel them staring as I entered the building. Like most people, I'd written off that part of town. I would drive through, never stop or get out of the car.

I put on a white butcher-style apron and started serving and clearing. It didn't take long for me to relax. I watched as bent-over and head-hanging men seated themselves on the chairs and long benches at the tables. Were they bent over from poor health, or from shame? Some couldn't even eat once they sat down and were served, and left plates nearly untouched.

I began to tolerate the stench that arose from some of Portland's unwashed. Each person had a story written with lines on his face and pain in his eyes. Many of these men had lost self-respect and dignity. Many would never leave skid road alive.

America is a country that has found the answers to so many questions on how to make life more pleasant, more comfortable— but hasn't found the answer to motivating men to lift themselves out of the gutter. It's a problem that's always been with us, and no doubt will continue to offend our senses.

Many people have been on skid road so long that it's home. They don't want to leave because they don't want what the world outside has to offer. They don't want to adjust and conform. Many can't leave because there's nowhere else for them to go. Some do get away, return to another part of society, another neighborhood.

I've gone back to Blanchet House to take pictures for a magazine article, and I still see the man in the long, gray overcoat as a shadow in my memory. I can't claim to have given much that Thanksgiving, but thank God for what I received.

His first name was Lincoln

It was an overcast, dull, cold Christmas Eve. An afternoon when I had plenty to do at home, and had difficulty explaining to my children why I wanted or needed to be out taking pictures and covering a news story.

A two-story, white peeled-paint frame house was set far back on the winter-barren acres. Gray smoke puffed out of the chimney. The driveway was muddy, and I hesitated entering—knowing how it could ice over and harden when the temperature dropped on a December, Oregon evening.

The rear wheels of an old black Chevy spun around as the Chicano behind the steering wheel. Accelerated and another boy, probably his brother, waved his arms frantically for him to stop as the rear wheels dug deeper into the mud.

The Presbyterian Church people stood on the front porch of the house as I approached with my camera and note pad—ready to record and intrude.

Members of the church group weren't looking for rewards or recognition when they "adopted" an indigent, migrant worker family with 12 children. I had to convince the church people they'd be doing a public service by letting the community know what they were doing. Perhaps motivate others to do similar deeds.

The story began one Sunday during the "Minute for Missions," when the pastor told his congregation about the Mexican-American family of 14. They slept on mattresses laid on the floors of a three-room cabin. When it rained the roof leaded and the mattresses soaked up the moisture like blotters. Winter cold was coming.

The response of the congregation was spontaneous. Enough families pledged funds to get the migrant-worker family through the winter months. There wasn't a formal committee for the purpose, those who were interested helped and it spread by word of mouth.

"We don't want to offer them pity—but love," said one of the churchwomen. "And, if you love people you care about their dignity." She was in charge of getting housing for the family, and that was an extremely difficult task.

Getting to know the family was all part of the plan. Not to impose upon them, but to let them know there was help available.

"It's not a matter of converting them to our church," the woman continued, "it's a matter of helping someone who needs help and caring about them." It was the pastor's wish that they not just give money, but follow through with a real concern for the family.

Finding housing proved inhibiting. The church people wanted the family to be comfortable, yet, to be able to handle part of the financial responsibility. A few days before Christmas they found a house that would be available until warmer weather. The wheels went into motion. The family liked the house but there was much work to be done.

Members of the Presbyterian Church spent a whole Sunday putting fresh paint on tired walls in the three bedrooms, while volunteers did a major repair job on the bathroom fixtures. The Senior High Youth Group voted to use the money in their treasury to take on one room as a project. They painted, made curtains, and did all the necessary work on their vacation time.

Church members received a list of the names and ages of the 12 children, with an appeal for Christmas gift clothing. New and used clothing poured in. Major furnishings like beds, crib, lamps, chairs, a stove, refrigerator and other necessities started rolling in.

At 4:00 p.m. Christmas Eve the pastor and four of the church members and their children brought the Christmas tree, decorations and gifts to the home of the Mexican-American family.

The lady of the house opened freshly painted and lined kitchen cupboards to display full shelves of food. She smiled and said, "you've already done so much for us," and took them through the other rooms in the house to show what had been done.

In one of the upstairs bedrooms a 13-year-old girl was sorting toys and clothing brought by one of the church members. She held out her soiled skirt and apologized, "We have been doing a lot of cleaning." The children of the church people knelt down on the floor beside the girl and helped her with the sorting, until they all became absorbed with an interesting storybook.

The Christmas tree was decorated and glittering when we came down to the living room. A two-year-old boy with large brown eyes and smooth, dark hair stared in awe at the tree and gifts. He watched everything with keen interest but didn't smile. He ran to his mother for reassurance. He admired the tree covered with handmade ornaments, left clinging to the branches when it was removed from the school classroom the day before.

I asked the mother if she could encourage her little boy, his name was Lincoln, to pose for a picture. He clung to her skirts and reached out with his right hand to receive the much larger, warm handshake of the man from the church. The moment I caught the look of the future on the face of the boy named Lincoln in my viewfinder, I pressed the lever to freeze him forever in my memory.

In the midst of "poverty" Lincoln experienced the love of his family and newly found friends. The room was warm with good things, and hope shone in the brightness of a little boy's eyes.

It was a misty-eyed drive home. I blinked at the headlights from the approaching cars on the highway and said out loud to nobody, "Merry Christmas," and went home and hugged my littlest children to their bewilderment.

Jeff was black and I *was* prejudiced

Too often the only time a person's name appears in the newspaper it's in the obituary column. There's more to life than that.

Jeff was a black student in our predominantly white suburban parochial school skirting the largest black housing project in Detroit.

We were in our senior year. Jeff was in another homeroom but we shared a class in Bible History. He sat in the desk at my right, halfway back in the third row from the windows.

He was a good student, a valuable asset on the school basketball team, well received by his fellow students and responsive to their friendship. Jeff was a tall, quiet boy with inner beauty that expressed itself in his warmth of character.

Yet, there was a barrier between Jeff and me. Barriers made me uncomfortable—especially when I had a strong hunch that I was the one responsible. People talked about prejudice, but I couldn't identify with the kind of racial hatred I grew up with in the Detroit area. I didn't feel any hatred for blacks, but definitely uneasy and fearful.

Prejudice can be little things. Like a black boy tugging at my pigtails from the desk behind when the first grade teacher is opening up a whole world of knowledge for me. It's running home from school because a black boy flashed a knife and started chasing. Teasing? I was too young to decide. It's seeing a little white girl cry and throw an ice cream cone away after a teasing little black girl took a lick and "made it dirty." It's hearing your mother quietly tell your brother to please not bring that little black boy home after school again—while the boy sits on the curb in front of the house waiting to play. It's being knocked down on the ice pond in the vacant lot by a black girl twice my age and size. It's living through the 1943 "race riots" where 23 blacks are killed and the city goes berserk with confusion, fear and hatred. It's gradually building up protective barriers because a few bad impressions by some representatives of a particular race refuse to vacate the memory.

I could detail even more real or imagined harm done to me by whites, but when you're building a prejudice your mind doesn't calculate that way. With the whites who harmed me it was a matter of the person and not the race—and I can remember what that individual did.

I never felt right or good about the prejudices compounding in me. They were subtle and I hid them well—from everyone but myself. I knew I couldn't live my whole lifetime being afraid of blacks, it hurt me too much. They really weren't aware of it.

If I could ever learn to know a black as a fellow human being it would have to be Jeff who would help me. I was still more of an observer than a participant in trying to overcome my particular fear and prejudice. Jeff, if he ever knew of my struggle never revealed it, but helped me by his quiet, warm person to learn to erase color of skin from the picture.

"Could I please borrow a piece a paper?" He asked across the aisle one day before a test began.

"Sure," I handed it across without hesitation.

And on another day I might ask him if he had the answer to one of the homework questions, and we would share our conclusions before class started. When you're a normal, healthy and active teenager in the senior year of school the prejudice problem doesn't occupy much of the waking or sleeping time. It was quickly relegated to the subconscious and left to resolve itself naturally in its own good time.

Over a period of time I could comfortably talk to Jeff about school activities and homework. Some of my friends double dated with Jeff and his girlfriend from his housing project. She went to a public school in Detroit. Some of my friends backslapped, joked and were loose and relaxed with Jeff. I still felt some barriers.

Suddenly, Jeff was stricken with leukemia. One day he was absent from the desk next to me in Bible History. We were counting the weeks until graduation, but Jeff never returned to that desk—or to any other desk. He was hospitalized for a series of tests.

One Sunday afternoon five of my close girlfriends got together with "nothing to do," and one proposed we take a bus trip to the hospital to visit Jeff. First we called to be sure we could visit. The hospital was strange territory for our little group, but we found our way to Jeff's room with help from a nurse who seemed pleased that we had come to visit.

The reports that came to us at school over the next several weeks and days made it look rather doubtful that Jeff would be attending graduation. We all put our spiritual force of prayer behind his wish to graduate with his class. We didn't know he would be there until we started walking up the church center aisle for the pomp and circumstance of graduation proceedings. There were two capped and gowned figures sitting in the front row to the right. One was a childhood sweetheart of mine. He'd been recovering from a serious illness and making a gallant comeback. We'd been praying for him as well as Jeff. The other boy is another story, and I'm here to talk about the black boy sitting next to him, Jeff.

I didn't look around to see if there were dry eyes that night, but I know much attention was focused on the two boys who came out of their sick beds to graduate.

With red, imitation leather-bound diplomas in hands, and

tassels turned to signify our advance, we marched out into the world and searched for our friends in the meeting rooms and parking lots.

It was a warm, early summer night. A group of graduates stood by the parking lot fence congratulating a smiling Jeff with gentle pats on the back and handshakes. As I approached the small group I observed that the girls ran up to the male classmates and planted graduation kisses on lips and cheeks. Jeff stood there, smiling his broad grin of white teeth against his black skin.

I walked directly to Jeff, held out my right hand for a congratulation handshake and leaned forward on my tiptoes and planted a kiss firmly on his right cheek.

"I'm so happy you're here, Jeff," I swallowed the hard lumps forming in my throat. "Thank you for coming." I couldn't tell if he blushed or beamed with pride. When he returned congratulations and said, "Thank you," so much human acceptance and Christian love was exchanged. I felt that somehow he knew what I had felt but never expressed.

Too often we regret those left-undone acts of love. As I look back I'm grateful I was able to cross the barrier I'd built. Able to show another person I cared. Grateful that person was so approachable.

Sixty-nine graduates went their separate ways. A very few weeks later a phone call informed me that Jeff died.

A small group of my close friends again boarded a bus to go and see Jeff. The funeral was at the Chapel of Our Lady of Victory, in a black neighborhood in Detroit.

The wood floor of the chapel creaked as we walked in, and my knees cracked, as they always did, when I genuflected at the pew. Black faces turned and viewed us. I thought for a moment we were out of place—but sorrow and mourning have colorless faces, and death is nondiscriminatory.

The prayers of blacks and whites went up in unison, remembering a human being who left his impression on our lives.

George True—to make a happy sound

Three college students selected Loaves and Fishes, a noontime hot meal program for the elderly, as an Advertising class project. We'd completed all of the research and done the preliminary promotional plan, then selected one of the centers to observe and take pictures for our slide presentation.

George True was the entertainment director at the senior citizen residence where we observed. Meeting and greeting was his pleasure, and he spread his warmth around the room at lunch time. The black man in his early 60s talked with me about his life in the entertainment field, and I gradually switched into my reporter's hat and started taking notes on the unused portion of my table napkin. Then returned at a later date to get the following story.

George True made his first drum from a wash tub and used spindle sticks from the back of an old chair as he taught himself to beat out rhythm.

"My family couldn't afford to get me drums," said True. He was the third oldest child in a family of 12 children living in Minneapolis, Minnesota, where his father was a chef at the Great Western Hotel.

"After I got a paper route I bought myself a used snare drum when I was 13. Then, someone admired my playing and bought me a set of drums when I was in high school." He never discovered the identity of his generous donor. Later he received offers from drum companies to use his name to advertise their product.

"My family wanted me to be a minister in the worst way," said True. But his interest in music and high school dramatics led him into the entertainment world. While still in high school he spent his spare time performing in nightclubs. His principal encouraged him to try to make a living at entertaining.

True went from a six-member group of musicians he pulled together in 1926 to a 16-piece dance band that played the Minnesota State Fair for 15 years. He played most of the East Coast, and the Pacific Northwest after moving to Portland in 1947. He's proud to mention names like Oscar Petaford and Lester Young who played in his Minneapolis dance band and went on to the "big time."

"Duke Ellington and Count Basey took most of my big musicians, and I told them to go ahead into the big time."

True first met his wife when they were both playing summer stock in North Dakota. He recalls that she was a Ziegfield Follies girl, Miss Minnesota in the late 30s, and a member of the Earl Carroll Reviews. She died in an auto accident while visiting in Minnesota in 1955. Their son John was an active entertainer in the Portland area before his move to the Los Angeles area where he carried on the musical tradition all the way to Las Vegas bookings.

The most colorful and dangerous period in George True's entertainment career was during the "Roaring 20s." It was a time when gangsterism, bootlegging and speakeasies in Minneapolis were financially profitable for musicians who played their instruments and "saw nothing."

True has a thin scar on his upper lip as a souvenir reminder of the night a bullet whizzed under his nose while he played drums— and he finished the number. One night a gangster broke up his whole set of drums "and another gangster found out about it and made the guy buy me a whole new set.

"The strangest thing that ever happened was when my trio had to sing over a gangster's body when he was in the casket. It was in his will for us to sing "Old Gang of Mine" while his friends drank. We sang it four times."

A command performance took place one night when a gangster held a gun to the head of one of the musicians and said "Play!"

"What do I do, George?" whispered the frightened musician. "I've got a family."

"I'm married, too," said George. "Just keep playing. They'll give us some money."

The gangster gave them $1,000. "The gangsters liked to throw their money around," said True. "And you had to be ready for anything."

George True's musicians played at Bond selling parades and rallies during World War II, then he served in the Merchant Marines from 1941 to 1946. After he settled in Portland he put a group of musicians together and began playing dances and clubs in the Pacific Northwest. He played all the leading clubs and in the private homes of some of the areas "finest citizens."

He's proud of his efforts in bringing Walter Bridges out of retirement to conduct the 15-piece "Jazz Festival Review" band that played at the Cotton Club in 1961, and during the Portland Rose Festival. The group played for the Rose Festival for six more years.

True, in semi-retirement, took his "True Bluers" trio wherever their agent books them. "But, I don't depend on music for income. I do it for fun." He devotes considerable time to being entertainment director of the senior citizen residence where he acts as official meeter and greeter for the Loaves and Fishes program in the building. He also acts as Master of Ceremonies for the social hour following lunch and draws attendance from outside the building.

"People are after me all the time for charity," said True. "It's part of my life and I continue right along. The good Lord's been good to me and I try to go along."

He was a counselor at an art center for two years and taught kids to play drums. He made contacts with kids who called him when they had problems. "The older musicians try to set a good example and keep the kids straight—a lot of them get into rock bands and on drugs.

"They think they can play better on drugs. But, if you're not good to start with all the drugs in the world won't make you good." True said that his policy with his own orchestra was always one of a decent life—Like Lawrence Welk."

He said he helped straighten out two of his own men with drug problems. "If a musician had a problem I always tried to counsel him. I told them that the only way to make it was to get rest, and if you're lonesome there's always a church near."

George True gently turns the pages of his scrapbooks and points to press clippings. "I was brought up in an old fashioned Baptist family. I learned respect for myself and for others. If I hadn't had a good set of values I would have ended up like some of the others. A dozen top musicians hit skid road and are now dead because they got hooked on drugs."

He recalls the night he overheard a teenage couple making a suicide pact when his band played a party in Eugene. At 1:00 a.m. the couple's car headed toward "Suicide Bridge" in Portland— unaware of another car following at a distance. True and three members of his band followed when the couple left the dance.

The couple listened to advice given to them on "Suicide Bridge" and in time overcame parental disapproval of their relationship. They're married now and George True treasures post cards and Christmas greetings they send.

How to achieve without really hearing

Steve Koopman leans forward and studies my face, particularly the movement of my lips. I strain for the attention to understand his laboriously formed words, realizing how dependent I am on my own ability to hear.

The sandy-hair, smiling high school senior with a 3.75 grade point average, and member of the Honor Society lives with his persistent mastery of the 85 percent hearing loss he's had since birth. Special hearing aids reduce that loss by 20 percent.

"The hearing person has to speak directly to me," Steve says as he sits on the edge of a living room chair and glances over at his mother. She smiles reassuringly and lets him handle the interview on his own. "Because I lip read and can't read the back of the head," he adds.

I gradually reach a comfort level as Steve studies the expression on my face while I listen to his response to my questions. I can't fake understanding because the puzzlement registers immediately on my face and he picks it up just as quickly.

"Many people hesitate to repeat," Mrs. Koopman offers one of her few comments, "or to say they don't understand. Steve would rather have them be honest." Although Mrs. Koopman remains for the most of the interview she insists that Steve answer the questions and express his own feelings. It becomes increasingly evident as to how Steve went beyond merely coping with a handicap and learned self-confidence, independence, achievement and excellence.

"My mother and father contributed a lot of help," said Steve, "and I appreciate that help." It was clear from talking with Steve and Mrs. Koopman that success did not come easily. There were years of hard work, patience and love poured into daily living for Steve to reach his present level of competence.

Steve attended his first training school in the State of Washington, followed by several years in California public school for the deaf. When the family moved to Oregon he received additional training at the Tucker-Maxin Oral School for the Deaf in Portland. During those two years he took public bus transportation and transferred each time without ever getting lost.

"He knows more about the downtown and the bus system than we do," commented Mrs. Koopman.

When the school for the deaf embarked on a joint integrated program, Steve attended the intermediate public school, and went on into high school.

"It helped me to get organized and to be with hearing kids," said Steve, in appreciation of the program. "Now I am with the hearing kids all day, except for one hour a day in English class." A specially trained teacher travels throughout the district and meets with students like Steve once a week.

Steve favors Math and it is where he gets his top grades. He does his Trigonometry homework at school during a study period so that he can devote after-school time to his 20-hour-a-week job in the kitchen of the local hospital.

Being financially independent is important to Steve. Although he drives the family car to and from work he boasts, "I pay my own insurance. There are four others in the family and my parents shouldn't have to pay that. It's too much money."

Steve lists his hobbies as traveling, bowling, bicycling and power mechanics where he overhauls lawnmowers. "I like to meet people and travel—in that combination," Steve beams as he opens a scrapbook filled with airline literature, post cards and pictures covering his 45-day European tour that took in eight countries. He was the only traveler in a group of 20 students and two leaders with a hearing problem. He said that he changed planes 15 times and the food in various countries was okay, except in Russia, where "it is very different."

He said that he learned something about this country after being in Europe. "America is the best place to live because I am most attuned to this way of life."

To Steve Koopman "this way of life" means paying his own way. He's proud of the fact that he's paying the full cost of his European holiday. "I still owe my parents about 30 percent of the amount. It was too much for them to pay. I wanted to do it."

Steve went on to study accounting, learn sign language so that he could communicate with deaf students who use only sign language. He served on the State Advisory Committee on Education for the Deaf, and continued to seek out the best methods available in providing total communication opportunities between the deaf and the hearing communities.

Marty Mann—a life without alcohol

Margaret "Marty" Mann was born October 15, 1904 and died July 22, 1980. Her introduction to Alcoholics Anonymous and its founders was in 1939, when her psychiatrist, Dr. Harry Tiebout, gave her a manuscript of the AA Big Book. She had three "slips" or "relapses" in her first 18 months in AA. Once sober she remained so until her death— shortly after addressing AA's 1980 International Convention in New Orleans. Although the National Council on Alcoholism, which she founded, was not connected with AA, she always gave credit to AA when and where it was due. I wrote the following story for the Portland Community Press, probably in or about the year 1972.

"Learning to live without alcohol in a world where you are surrounded by it requires a complete re-education process," said

Marty Mann, founder of and consul to the National Council on Alcoholism."

Since Mrs. Mann began her recovery from the disease of alcoholism in 1939 she has written two books: *New Primer on Alcoholism* and *Marty Mann Answers Your Questions about Drinking and Alcoholism*. During the Seventies, when this interview took place, Marty Mann was averaging 200 lectures a year throughout the United States.

Following her training at the Yale School of Alcohol Studies in 1944, Mrs. Mann founded the National Council on Alcoholism and began lecturing. She focused on three basic concepts: 1.) Alcoholism is a disease and the alcoholic is a sick person. 2.) The alcoholic can be helped and is worth helping. 3.) This is a public health problem and therefore a public responsibility."

In support of this view of alcoholism as a treatable disease the American Medical Association officially declared it a disease and medical responsibility in 1956.

"There has been great progress in treating alcoholism as a disease," said Mrs. Mann. "In 1944 there were no facilities. The first two in the country opened on an experimental basis a month before I founded the National Council on Alcoholism. At that time Alcoholics Anonymous had 10,000 members. They have over 500,000 today. Now, 60 percent of the general hospitals will accept alcoholics for treatment." (Half a million in 1970 something. Several millions now.)

Mrs. Mann said that the variety of treatment facilities as well as Alcoholics Anonymous, out-patient care, hospitalization and psychiatric counseling all serve a particular need in the community. The only instance mentioned as harmful treatment was in the case of "trying to teach an alcoholic to drink successfully. It doesn't work." She cited Antabuse (medication and adjunct to treatment) as a major contribution discovered in 1949.

"It (Antabuse) builds up a chemical fence to keep the alcoholic sober long enough to get his mind working," she said. Antabuse causes a violent reaction when combined with alcohol, therefore alcohol must be avoided.

"The waterfront has been well covered," said Mrs. Mann. "There are more facilities for treating the derelict and court offender representing three percent of the alcoholics than there are for the 97 percent in the middle or upper class." She said that doctors are reluctant to tell patients they are alcoholics because of the stigma attached, and that patients "don't come clean" with their doctors.

"There is not nearly enough cooperation between different groups doing things in the area of alcoholism," said Mrs. Mann. "This is understandable because we were all understaffed and overworked in the beginning, and each one was interested in his own progress. We are just beginning to make the effort to combine."

She said that when these groups get together and share experiences they can avoid making some of the same mistakes and avoid lost time in referring alcoholics and their families to the wrong agency.

"This is the whole purpose of the Council on Alcoholism in a community. I call it the hub of the wheel," said Mrs. Mann. "We can determine the referral by what he needs, what he is able to pay, and what will succeed for him."

Mrs. Mann said that industry is the key area for success with the alcoholic. "Industry has the best motivating tool to treatment. It is easier to treat him while still employed and before too much damage is done. Four and a half million alcoholics are employed on every level from the night watchman to the president of the company."

Mrs. Mann said that insurance companies have discovered they have gained, not lost, as a result of including alcoholic treatment in their policies. Management can get the coverage for employees, and early treatment will prevent loss of work and medical expense for vague illness like "gastritis and fatigue.

"There are 250 major corporations with an employee alcohol program, including the Federal Government. (Mid-70s statistics.)

The Civil Service commission hired a man from the National Council on Alcoholism to head up their program. The Department of the Interior and Post Office have long had programs, but it is now required throughout government agencies as a result of the Hughes Bill passed in early 1971.

When asked if there was a need for more recovered alcoholics to go public Mrs. Mann said there were only two others "Telling the whole world they are recovered alcoholics." She said that not many were willing to risk the effects of the stigma still attached to the disease. "Everyone has some pre-conceived idea that alcoholics are bad, weak willed, lacking in character, and a little less than human."

Mrs. Mann said that passage of the Uniform Act would take alcoholism out of the criminal category and place it in the health category. She cited this as a major step in getting proper treatment to the right place at the right time when alcoholics are legally retained.

Major steps in Federal funding in the field of alcoholism treatment and research have come through the National Institute on Alcohol Abuse, and are in the process of evaluating programs submitted by the individual states applying for part of the 30 million dollars earmarked for formula grants. These funds are supposed to pick up where the Department of Transportation funded programs for better law enforcement with the drinking driver leave off. The Department of Transportation programs are intended to identify and diagnose, the National Institute funds will go into the area of treatment.

In 1944, when Marty Mann founded the National Council on Alcoholism there were an estimated three million alcoholics in the United States. By the mid-1970s, the number rose to nine million. It only increases through the decades.

Although advances have been made in the area of treatment, Marty Mann said, "the biggest problem we have is that we do not know the causes." And she looked forward to advances in the area of prevention through public information and community education.

The collective battered child

The following story was published in 1969. Although it references a particular county in Oregon—the statistics are no longer relevant and the people quoted probably are no longer in those positions—the importance of the concepts and information make it worth repeating.

Statistics do not always reveal the true picture. This seems to be the case in the matter of the "battered child" problem.

Battered children, under the age of 12, are brought to the attention of the authorities in various ways when it becomes evident that they have suffered physical harm from blows, beatings, physical violence, or neglect deliberately inflicted.

Those who are in the position of dealing directly with battered children feel the problem goes much deeper than their written reports. All of those I interviewed expressed the wish to see the child stay in the home, recognizing the delicate nature of the problem with child and parent relationships.

There were only about ten "battered child" cases recorded in Washington County during 1968. In one case a store owner called the Juvenile Department when two small children were seen wandering around the parking lot in poor physical condition. A father had lost his temper. This was against his nature and he needed help. Through counseling he received the help he needed and the children remained in their own home.

"Many people do not know what to do," said Ruby Ellis when referring to the cases that never come to her attention in the Washington County Juvenile Department. She went on to explain the way her department works in cooperation with the Welfare Department, Tualatin Valley Guidance Clinic, the Health Department, and other agencies. Emphasis is on the "health and welfare of the child" and the "feeling that the family should remain intact wherever possible."

Because of the delicate nature of the problem, many people are reluctant to report a "battered child" situation when it comes to their attention.

"We will not take action on anonymous calls," said Mrs. Ellis. "but, we assure the person who calls that their name will not be revealed." There are, of course, times that a report may be unfounded upon investigation. Even so, Mrs. Ellis feels that it is necessary for people to have an increased "concern for children who can't take care of themselves."

There are certain steps that are taken in the case of the "battered child" that come to the attention of authorities. Referral can come from any source, such as, the school, a relative, neighbor, or interested citizen. The initial report may come to the attention of the city or county law enforcement agency, the Juvenile, Welfare or Health Departments.

Any referral must then be immediately turned over to the Washington County Health Department.

If upon investigation evidence is found, then the matter is turned over to the District Attorney.

The matter is then brought before the Juvenile Circuit Judge within 24 hours to determine whether the situation requires authorization to have the child remain outside the home for a time. Then the District Attorney determines if prosecution is in order against the adult(s) involved in the ill treatment.

Dr. James Stewart, head of the Washington County Health Department, admits that the agencies involved sometimes become excessively timid because it is a serious step, "and we are loath to interfere with parental rights." He went on to stress the need of removing the child temporarily from the "high risk situation" while it is still under study.

"What we need and hope to do," said Dr. Stewart, "is get a better focus on the welfare of the child and not be, as previously, concerned with the question, is or isn't the parent guilty. If the child is in a home in need of study—then we must do what is in the best interest of the child."

Helen Patterson, Child Welfare Supervisor in Washington County, expressed the regret that in many cases "our hands are tied in wanting to protect the child in a case of suspected abuse." This results from the need for sufficient information and evidence to make a legal case. "All agencies involved in the matter of the battered child," she said, "are very much aware of the letter of the law."

Captain Donald Jones of the Beaverton Police Department reported only two cases falling into the "battered child" category during 1968 (with one being referred back to Multnomah County where there was a previous offense.)

"It's a family type situation," said Capt. Jones, "one parent does not report another parent. Then the child is taken to the doctor, and you have a doctor-patient problem where they are reluctant to make a report."

As a result of passage of an Oregon State law two years ago, doctors and interns are given immunity from liability if they should report a suspected case of child abuse which later proves to be unfounded. They also are required by state law to report cases where they believe a child under 12 has suffered bodily harm as the result of deliberate blows or battering.

What type of person would inflict bodily harm on their own child? The neurotic, the psychotic, one who looses balance or restraint, one who is deeply disturbed and takes out aggressive tendencies in violence? The problem ignores social and economic boundaries and can enter the sphere of the indigent, as well as the affluent.

A prominent pediatrician in the area remarked that it wasn't too common for a doctor in practice to come across cases of severe child beating. In most cases the parents are ashamed to bring them in to the office. He said that their concern was more in prevention. When a parent brings a child into the office and is obviously under tension and agitated, an attempt is made to reassure the parent and improve their relationship with the child.

The pediatrician agreed that there are far more incidents than ever come to the attention of authorities. He gave an example of a woman who called her physician to the home to examine her young child who had suffered severe bruises. She was quite vague. Upon examination the doctor asked how it happened.

"I'm so relieved that you asked," she said. "I did it." She needed help, knew she needed help, but didn't know how to ask.

Run-a-way, who?

The following story was published in 1968. Although it references a particular county in Oregon—the statistics are no longer relevant and the people quoted probably are no longer in those positions—the importance of the concepts and information make it worth repeating.

Two hundred and fifty more juveniles have been referred to the Washington County Juvenile Department in the first six months of 1968 that for the corresponding period of 1967.

Based on information provided by Jerry M. Harkins, Director of the Juvenile Department for Washington County.

"The major offense is the runaway. Runaways have increased by 100 for the first six months of 1968." Harkins said that the majority involved girls in the 14- to 15-year-old age group, and boys in the 15 to 16 age group.

When asked if runaways became an increased problem during the school year, Harkins said, "It gives them more time to get away and more opportunity. Parents are letting children go without any real knowledge of where they are. When the child fails to return the next day (after staying overnight with a friend) you often discover that two are gone." The child and the friend.

"If they leave the metropolitan area they usually head for California and the 'Hippie' community. The reason for the increase," said Harkins, "is that it is easier for kids to obtain food, lodging and transportation. If they are hitchhiking and picked up by one of the 'Hippie' crowd, they are absorbed into the community and taken care of, then become involved in further and more serious offenses such as drugs."

Commenting on the use of drugs, Harkins said, "The referrals to the court for drug offenses in no way reflect the number of users. It is difficult to acquire evidence for conviction on drug use. We usually get them on the runaway charge."

"Most kids get involved in drug use by trying to experiment," he added. "Addicts start out on marijuana or dangerous drugs, but it does not follow through that someone who has used drugs will become an addict, anymore than a person who drinks beer will become an alcoholic—but, it increases the possibility."

Not every child who commits a delinquent act is a delinquent, according to a pamphlet published by the Department of Youth Authority State of California. "Most of the children involved in minor delinquencies are first-time, last-time offenders. Less than one percent of our youth will become sufficiently delinquent to require removal from their own homes."

Juvenile Delinquency is a term that has come to mean many things to many people. Children's cases are listed according to type of delinquency in Washington County. They range from the runaways which numbered 516 in 1967 to the curfew violations which numbered 286 for that time. Other offenses included the possessing and drinking of liquor involving 286, and truancy or school problems at 97. Shoplifting, and/or cases of larceny, and breaking and entering presented a combined total of 486 among juveniles in 1967, with 276 for the first six months of 1968. Unauthorized use of car ranks high of 91 for 1967 and 33 recorded for the first six months of 1967.

According to Harkins, a child who resides and is cited in Washington County (and sometimes those cited in Multnomah County) appears in the adult court for driving violations and it is an accumulation of citations that brings him before the Juvenile Court where he loses his license for a time. There is an example of a youth who accumulated seven citations in 18 months: hitchhiking, disregarding a stop sign (twice), violation of basic rule (speed) twice, unnecessary noise (tire squealing), and failure to yield the right away. The youth will probably lose the right to drive for a year or more.

Adult courts have definite set penalties for offenses, but in the Juvenile Court there is a flexibility that depends upon the individual child, and what is best for him. The basic philosophy of the Juvenile Department is Chapter 419 of the Oregon Revised Statute:

"Provision of ORS 419.472 to 419.587 shall be liberally construed to the end that a child coming within the jurisdiction of the court may receive such care, guidance, and control, preferably in his own home, as will lead to the child's welfare and the best interests of the public, and that when a child is removed from the control of his parents the court may secure for him care that best meets the need of the child"

Many times the juvenile (age up to 18 years but not inclusive) is unaware of the consequences that may result from what seems to be a joke or rather harmless. There is the example of the boy who was given LSD in a soft drink. A joke that resulted in serious injury to the boy. The girl who was given seeds from a common plant that produces an intoxicating effect. She was taken into custody and exposed their prank for what it really was.

A "lookout" is just as much involved as the person who commits the offense. Theoretically, hitchhiking could carry the same penalty as shoplifting or taking a car. But, here again the disposition is based on the child as an individual. Draping a friends house and shrubbery with toilet paper is an innocent prank to be compared with the "raiding of pumpkin patches and overturning of outhouses," according to Harkins. But again, theoretically, it might involve a visit from a representative of the Juvenile Department to counsel the child and family regarding private property and where pranks sometimes lead.

"It is most important," said Harkins, "for parents to know where their children are, the same as it is important for children to know where parents are. Trusting your children does not mean you do not check that they are where they are supposed to be. Not every time, but occasionally.

"Parents need to communicate more within the family, as well as with the parents of their children's friends," Harkins added. "All kids need different limits. What is right for one is not necessarily right for another. Not all people need the same rule, and this may differ from family to family, as well as from child to child within the same family. A rule based solely on age is not justifiable."

When asked again what he thought caused children to run away from home, Harkins said, "Inconsistency to follow through. There is a need for sincerity. If parents threaten to punish then they should carry out their threat. Otherwise it is a sign of weakness, and when they do eventually carry out the threat after repeated warnings it is a sign of previous insincerity. When a parent threatens, 'the next time you do that,' the next time should bring the punishment. They interpret leniency as not caring. They can also interpret strictness as over-protectiveness, so there is a need for sincerity."

Many children become delinquents long before they come under the jurisdiction of the court or Juvenile Department. According to the pamphlet published by the Department of Youth Authority State of California:

"Delinquents don't just happen. They are the product of circumstances, chance, culture and environment, and most importantly, psychological conditioning.

"There is a small number of youth who acquire the label of delinquent by circumstance. Frequently the young person who commits a delinquent act under these circumstances is a member of a group that engages in unlawful behavior temporarily. It is the presence and pressure of his friends and associates that helps him commit an act that he knows to be wrong.

"There are children who grow up in an area of crime and vice until it becomes their way of life, and they see nothing wrong with it. He is the cultural delinquent and has a greater opportunity to get into trouble. His potential as a delinquent is higher.

Certain children have been psychologically conditioned to have a higher delinquency potential. "In this group," continues the pamphlet, "we have children who have had everything they did or said disapproved. Every effort has been made to make them feel inferior. Parents have denied them admiration, appreciation, and affection, and have permitted boredom to be a constant companion. Adults have taken every opportunity to show suspicion and disbelief. They have had parents who have never let them forget who is the boss. Such children tend to show marked characteristics as a potential delinquent.

"He is socially aggressive and shows extremes in defiance, suspicion, and destructiveness. He is suggestible and easily led by children in his own group when he accepts them as his authority. With adults and others in authority, he is frequently stubborn. It is the extent and duration of these deviations that establish delinquency, not just a single unusual or illegal action by a child."

The pamphlet goes back to what Director of the Juvenile Department, Harkins, said regarding prevention beginning in the home. The importance of knowing your child and what he is going through. Knowing his assets, as well as his liabilities. Trying to understand why he acts the way he does. Helping him work out his problems on his own. Giving him a chance to express himself and release his energy. Letting him develop his individual personality without trying to make him like someone else. Keeping discipline consistent, humane, and in the right spirit.

During the first six months of 1968 there were 1062 boys and 356 girls brought before the Washington County Juvenile Department.

Numbers and statistics do not reflect the extent of the growing problem that faces the individual, the parents, the law enforcement agencies, and the community as a whole. Nor do the statistics reflect the thousands of good kids who never become a problem to society as delinquents. Thousands of "unsung heroes and heroines" in Washington County, and every other county in the country who make the extra effort to "hold the line" and stay in line.

Remember to remember

" . . . that these dead shall not have died in vain . . . "

The hope of our nation was expressed in these words by President Abraham Lincoln at Gettysburg, field of battle and grave for the dead soldiers of North and South, in 1863.

May 30 was a date chosen by some Southern women to decorate the graves of Union and Confederate armies. The May 30 date may have been chosen by Cassandra Oliver Moncure, one of the Southern ladies of French origin. In France, May 30 was "The Day of the Ashes" commemorating the return of Napoleon's remains to France from St. Helena.

In 1868, Major General John A. Logan named May 30 as a day of honoring the graves of Union soldiers. A group of Union veterans organized Memorial Day celebrations until the American Legion assumed the duties after World War I.

Memorials have been cast in stone, written for history, sung from reviewing stands, placed on graves, and remembered in hearts aching still with grief.

America's freedom from foreign power was born in its moment of decision and won on a battlefield. America has stretched, almost to the breaking point, her concern for the freedom of other nations—other brothers in the human family.

Our soldiers began to die on domestic battlefields for domestic causes, but so much American blood cries out to us from foreign land—asking us to consider whether these dead have died in vain.

As a nation we differ in our views of what constitutes a just war—but as a nation we should be united in honoring those who have fought and died on foreign or domestic soil.

God knows, we owe them that much!

American blood is still being spilled on domestic soil. We view with mixed emotions the outcries of our young people when they ask out for "peace" and beg for our servicemen to return. But on occasion we question whether demonstrations leading to violence and killing can possibly be the answer to getting favorable results.

Peace must start within the individuals. Anarchy in the streets does not constitute peace. We are heading for another summer that may again become one of those "long hot summers" that we have already experienced—and already forgotten. Summers of rioting, burning and killing—"can this nation long endure?"

We talk of peace and just wars, and just causes—and most of us find positions indefensible by both hawks and doves. We have had our hearts in our mouths too long over the Vietnam War and we are once again returning to the "brother against brother" war on the domestic soil.

Our country needs a house cleaning, for a "house so divided cannot long endure."

Men and women of America have entered service to their country and died without knowing fully why. We, the living, can give them no good reasons. There are no good reasons for war— only conscientious dictates of necessity with the hope of overcoming some particular evil with the replacement of something better. Something hoped for that will justify all the lost lives.

This nation was not born without labor pains. Lives, honor and fortunes were lost in the delivery room. Only history can be the true judge of just causes. We enjoy the benefits of our American freedom compared to the slavery of other nations of the world, so we would have to admit that "those lives were not lost in vain."

In honoring our dead let us not examine the causes and results of the battle, but rather the integrity of the human person who did what he was told to do, or what he felt he had to do—to make this a better world.

How do we honor them? Flowers on the grave, tears of remembrance, prayers of hope for "No more war! As expressed by Pope Paul at the United Nations, a kind act or word in remembrance of one who died expressing hope for peace. However we remember—let us at least remember!

VIII

WHO AM I? AND WHO CARES?

The following short pieces were written in answer to a list of questions a friend of mine gave me to help free up my writer's block at that time. The thinking behind the questions is that we can't write about anything until we have a fair idea of who we are as individuals. Although this philosophical exercise was done many, many years ago I believe others may benefit from asking themselves a similar set of questions—and discovering where that takes them. I re-read these pages because they were in an envelope and tucked in with the manuscript you have just read. I am no longer certain of their significance, but thought the information was worth adding a chapter. For me, some of these statements also serve as affirmations, so I don't forget who I think I am. So here goes, with what used to be called "armchair philosophy."

Where do I fit in as a writer?

Writing is something I want to do and have to do in some form or another. I'm vain enough to think that my interpretation of my experiences in life is important enough to share with readers. Hopefully you will gain something from this shared experience. I consider myself a person who is whole and complete, not a woman who happens to be a writer, not a wife or mother who happens to be a writer—but a person who is compelled to share life by writing about it. I fit in because I believe in me and what I can do. I believe in the powers that move me. I can fit anywhere I want to if I make up my mind that I want to do something.

What kind of a person am I?

I guess I am a deep thinker. I must find some way of understanding, of accepting what happens around me. I must make sense somehow out of all the confusion. I am concerned with people but don't want to get overly involved because then I lose my perspective. I have difficulty separating the humanitarian from the writer. I feel that I can better serve at times by internalizing and writing rather than venting the emotion and performing some task. I'm reluctant to have anyone get so close to me that I lose touch with my inner thoughts. Some of them are sacred and meant to be shared on paper.

Am I a defender of the past?

I am more an explorer of the past. I want to understand what has gone before in order to find out what is happening now. The past interests me only as it relates to the present. It is a link in the long chain of events that has led to today. I am very interested in finding out why today is the way it is. How can a person defend the past. The past is. It is finished and its history has been written. We can only look at it and hopefully learn something from past events.

Am I a defender of the present?

Everything changes. Transition is occurring spontaneously, constantly around and within me. Even as I am writing, changes are occurring. I am aging. Tissue is changing. My brain is growing in power by the knowledge I am recycling into it at this moment. I am taking thoughts already in my head and putting them together in some kind of order with other thoughts from another part of my brain and making some kind of sense or logic of the whole thing. I think it is absolutely amazing and I am intoxicated with the whole damn process.

The present becomes past very quickly. So why defend it. God knows how to judge people. We know nothing about such matters, and know very little about judging events, as we are a part of them. So why defend. Keep on moving into the future. Try to learn as we go along. Adding piece after piece to the gigantic puzzle that we call the history of mankind. Someday the present will make sense. But for the present, we can only make sense out of a very small part of that whole. Yet, our role is to try to make sense out of the minute so we can contribute to the whole.

Or do I want to change the future?

Doesn't everyone! Why live if we can't see some possibility for a better life. Everyone perceives that "better" in a different way. That's what creates the Babel-ish confusion, with everyone doing what they think will move the course of history in the right direction according to their plan. I want to change the future. But so does everyone else. Leadership is a difficult thing to assess. Leaders are appointed by those who recognize their power to sway people in one direction or another. Enough people following a leader going in the same direction can accomplish something worthwhile. When we find the best vehicle for accomplishing the good we intend, then we should be on our way. Writing is one way I can change the future, by forcing people to look at the present—which will soon be past. The other is to have an influence personally on the people around me so that they in turn can influence the future—that's called leadership.

What is my particular talent?

People have told me that I am a leader. Maybe! I have a tendency to speak with a kind of conviction that makes people either nod their heads in agreement or shake them in rebellion. I intend to stir up the thinking person to examine and rethink. I have been told that I create a strong feeling of identification in my writing. I write like I talk. I talk like I think. It has become an easy flow. I have discovered the music within myself and I want to keep playing it until people hum along with me. I have a drive to finish what I start. I love to see something start from a spark of an idea and build slowly, painfully, over a period of time into a piece that can be shared with others. I feel like shouting "Look, I have put together something so unique that you may never see it done again in quite the same way. Sit up and take notice of what has come out of my head, my life, through my eyes—by putting it together with the power I call my God—and now I give it to you to examine. It is precious to me, hopefully it will be important to you—something to add to your life and use as a stepping stone to another idea that will make your life more worthwhile."

I have an insatiable curiosity about life and every thing, and everyone I meet.

What do I know about writers' markets?

I have spent a great deal of time exploring markets for writing. I have published in local, national and Canadian newspapers and magazines. In colleges, I have taught writing, editing, advertising, public relations, marketing and events planning. I keep up with trends by reading writers' magazines. I talk with other writers, and occasionally go to writers conferences. I read fiction and non-fiction for research and pleasure. I have continued to keep a journal since the 1960s. I'm always alert to good stories. I know the articles markets and have now chosen to work on book length material as well.

What do I read and enjoy?

Since 1964, I have kept a running list of books that I have read. When I finish a book I list it on the inside cover of my current journal. Later, I add the information to my computer generated list. Generally, I am reading one fiction and one non-fiction book, plus several periodicals and newspapers. I like biographies. I enjoy reading about new ways to solve social problems. I learn something from everything I read. I want to know more about the inner workings of the human mind and the individual's ways of interacting with nature and other humans. I'm interested in strong characters in fiction. Historical fiction teaches me something about the times and the people. In the past I read most of Irving Stone's historical fiction. I read most of the same modern day writers as everyone else. When we travel we listen to books on tape in the RV or the car. I like variety. I've read Rod McKuen's verse, Peanuts and Doonsbury comics, E.E. Cummings, and Edgar Allen Poe, etc., etc.

Am I prepared to face the truth about myself?

I have looked in the mirror and found it painful but worth the effort. I have had to accept the fact that others have told me I am a worthwhile person. I have achieved some degree of success and am moving too fast to know exactly what's happening.

Am I prepared to make changes?

I welcome change. I hate to remain staid or static. I don't want to be predictable. I want to live a better life, give others more of me. I can only continue to live by growing mentally, spiritually and emotionally. I gain so much from other people and hope by changing for the better that I can increase the value of my existence.

Am I prepared to sit on the fence and see both sides?

I want to observe both sides. I try to get into the skin of people who interest me. I want to walk in the Indian's moccasins and in the snow shoes of the Eskimo. I want to see how they live life. I see my side of an issue but want to try to understand what makes the other guy tick. BUT, I want to take a stand and not be a blur. I am not an "I don't know" person. I form definite opinions. They are my opinions—at least for the present. Tomorrow they may change and that is my privilege. I permit others to change as well.

What are my faults?

I still care a great deal about what others think of me and what I write. I want to be independent of needing supportive criticism but I don't think it is meant to be. I am sensitive to negative criticism. I am outspoken and often don't give the other person enough time to express himself. Sometimes the world moves too slow. I become impatient with people who aren't doing what I think they should be doing. Sometimes they take too long to say what it is they want to say. Sometimes I take too long as well. When I was young, I ran and leapt through life, but now, aging has slowed everything down to a walk or a stroll.

In the past I didn't want the kind of success where I would stand out in a crowd and be noticed. I guess I have learned to handle whatever comes my way. Come what may. I've finally learned to accept a compliment, and to give one. I'm more trusting of others and appreciate the good they bring into my life.

What can I do about my faults?

Accept the advice of the good critics who see me better than I see myself. Change when and where I can. Recognize the fault and act upon it as soon as possible. Be better organized. Set my schedule for writing so that I can get more done. Follow through!

What are the things I worry about?

I used to worry because I thought that would help solve the problem. I don't think that way any more. The things I listed that I worried about back in the Seventies no longer matter. Things I worried about yesterday no longer matter. I recall a scripture passage that says something about today's worries being sufficient unto themselves. Like—why worry? Be happy!